VOCATIONAL TRAINING
AND EMPLOYMENT OF THE
MODERATELY AND SEVERELY
HANDICAPPED AND AUTISTIC
ADOLESCENT
WITH PARTICULAR EMPHASIS
TO BILINGUAL
SPECIAL EDUCATION

VOCATIONAL TRAINING AND EMPLOYMENT OF THE MODERATELY AND SEVERELY HANDICAPPED AND AUTISTIC ADOLESCENT WITH PARTICULAR EMPHASIS TO BILINGUAL SPECIAL EDUCATION

By

ELVA DURÁN, PH.D.

California State University
Sacramento

Foreword by
Lou Brown, PH.D.
University of Wisconsin
Madison

CHARLES C THOMAS • PUBLISHER
Springfield • Illinois • U.S.A.

Published and Distributed Throughout the World by

CHARLES C THOMAS • PUBLISHER
2600 South First Street
Springfield, Illinois 62794-9265

© *1992 by* CHARLES C THOMAS • PUBLISHER

ISBN 0-398-05801-6

Library of Congress Catalog Card Number: 92-4817

With THOMAS BOOKS *careful attention is given to all details of manufacturing and design. It is the Publisher's desire to present books that are satisfactory as to their physical qualities and artistic possibilities and appropriate for their particular use.* THOMAS BOOKS *will be true to those laws of quality that assure a good name and good will.*

Printed in the United States of America
SC-R-3

Library of Congress Cataloging-in-Publication Data

Durán, Elva.
    Vocational training and employment of the moderately and severely handicapped and autistic adolescent with particular emphasis to bilingual special education / by Elva Durán ; foreword by Lou Brown.
        p.   cm.
    Includes bibliographical references (p.   ) and index.
    ISBN 0-398-05801-6
    1. Handicapped youth—Vocational education—United States.
2. Autistic youth—Education—United States.   3. Handicapped youth—Employment—United States.   4. Autistic youth—Employment—United States.   5. Bilingual education—United States.   I. Title.
LC4019.7.D87   1992
371.91—dc20   92-4817
                                                                                    CIP

CONTRIBUTORS

Lou Brown, Ph.D., Professor, Department of Rehabilitation Psychology and Special Education, University at Wisconsin at Madison who contributed the Foreword of this book.

Hyun-Sook Park, Ph.D., Assistant Professor, Department of Rehabilitation Psychology and Special Education, California State University, Sacramento, who contributed a chapter in this book. Dr. Park researches and specializes in the area of social skill training for persons with severe intellectual disabilities.

Marlene Simon, Phyllis Tappe, doctoral candidates at University at the California, Berkeley and **Thom Wozniah,** doctoral candidate, who also assisted Hyun-Sook Park in writing the chapter on Social Acceptance which appears in this book.

In memory of
Ed Ekwall

Dedicated to
Ruth Waugh, Ph.D.,
who has never tired of
guiding me through the years.

FOREWORD

Ideologically, i.e., when guided by beliefs as to what is fair, good, right and consistent with values and first principles, individuals with disabilities have the right to experience as many integrated components of society as anyone else.

Legally, i.e., when guided by the spirit of the U.S. Constitution, the Civil Rights Act of 1963, The Individuals and Disabilities Education Act of 1991 and the American's with Disabilities Act of 1990, the segregation or exclusion of individuals with disabilities from society can no longer be tolerated.

Many parents and professionals have now concluded that the positive limits of segregated service models have been reached. That is, resource rich state of the art program were able to accomplish as much as can be expected when individuals with disabilities were confined to segregated settings.

Armed with powerful ideological, legal and experiential arsenals, parents and professionals are now advocating, demanding and arranging that more and more persons with disabilities function in the same environments in which they would function if they were not disabled. However, while increasing numbers of such persons are "placed," "based" or "allowed to function" in integrated settings, relatively few are receiving meaningful and appropriate services therein. Unfortunately, ideology and law are more advanced than professional practice.

Historically, the technologies developed for use with individuals with intellectual disabilities have been determined by the environments in which they functioned. When warehoused in large "state institutions," the technologies necessary to manage or control them therein were developed. When confined to handicapped schools, special education classes, activity centers, sheltered workshops and other segregated settings "in the community," instructional and management technologies specific to those settings evolved.

When individuals with severe intellectual disabilities were first allowed access to integrated work environments, it was not known how to arrange for them to be productive therein. We know now. The point is that the technologies needed to engender successful functioning in integrated work environments could not have been developed until workers with disabilities were given reasonable opportunities to learn to function in them.

The contributions of Elva Durán and her associates that are recorded in this book will enhance the integration of persons with disabilities in our society. Those of us who know Elva are constantly amazed and humbled by her dedication, commitment and effectiveness. This book can be considered another brick in the house of peace and equality she is helping to build for persons with disabilities. Once again, I salute her.

Lou Brown

PREFACE

Presently there are few if any books which explain how to actually organize vocational training programs in the classroom. As this writer has been working in the field of placing students with severe autism and other intellectual disabilities to work she would hear various presenters say how people with disabilities should be placed in the community to work. By placing students to work in the community she has learned some practical information that should be helpful to teachers, job trainers, and parents.

Also, there are very few articles or materials that address the student with autism. This is a very neglected group of students. Again, as this writer has worked in the field with students with autism she has learned some things which may be helpful to parents and teachers. Students with autism have been this writer's greatest challenge and best teachers.

What this writer is most proud of all is the information she has included on bilingual methods. She spent several weeks researching this information in the library and talking to various bilingual education professors to get the techniques which could be and are useful in teaching students with severe handicaps who are limited English proficient. This was not easy as few materials are clearly and simply written which give examples and explain how to actually use bilingual methods to teach students who are second language learners or also are referred to as limited English proficient students.

This is the *first* book in special or bilingual education which explains how the bilingual methods could be used with students with *severe* handicaps who are limited English proficient.

It is the hope of this writer that these first efforts she has done in this book to bring practical information in the area of vocational training and it is her hope that the information she included which can be used with the language minority students will be helpful to many teachers and parents. This writer is committed to this area of providing language minority students in special education and students who have severe intellectual disabilities the best possible education. This writer will continue her efforts in these areas and in other practical areas which can be helpful to teachers who work with second language or language minority students who also have severe disabilities.

ELVA DURÁN

INTRODUCTION

Since the time of the Morrill Act of 1882, which helped states through-out the country recognize that some land could be set aside to develop vocational educational colleges; there has been an emphasis on provid-ing vocational education services to persons with intellectual disabilities. Another cornerstone which gave persons with intellectual disabilities a beginning in the area of vocational education was the Smith Hughes Act of 1917. This Act is often cited as another landmark beginning of train-ing and retraining of services for persons with disabilities.

Because of these laws and also many of the vocational rehabilitation amendments, persons with intellectual disabilities have started to make progress in helping people in the community accept that they can work.

Through the years, the work of Marc Gold in the seventies taught all of us for the first time that persons with severe disabilities could do more tasks than we even believed possible. With his task analysis system he was able to get persons with severe disabilities to assemble objects, bicycle brakes, etc. These particular operations required several steps and with patience and precision Marc Gold taught the adults how to be successful in all that they performed in the workplace.

The work of Lou Brown in the eighties and nineties helped carry Marc Gold's philosophy even a step or two further as he proposed that many of the students and adults could be trained to find work in the community. The concepts of people with disabilities being placed in the community becomes more and more prevalent and far reaching. Lou Brown assisted people with disabilities to get jobs in the community and called the jobs non-sheltered employment.

Other individuals like Thomas Bellamy and Robert Horner who trained several people with severe intellectual disabilities who come directly from state hospitals accomplished the major tasks of putting people to work who had never been trained nor had they seen much beyond the state hospital walls.

Non-sheltered vocational training for people with severe intellectual disabilities as well as those individuals who were also severe in nature but who had not been outside of state hospitals was more and more common.

The federal government started to place further emphasis and federal dollars on more programming to be accomplished for training and placing persons with severe disabilities in jobs in the community. Soon work like that of Paul Wehman became more well known because he was able to demonstrate again and again with the aid of federal monies that persons with severe intellectual disabilities could work in the community for pay.

More federal monies continued to be allocated and soon funds for yet another major movement for vocational education for persons with severe intellectual disabilities was yet to come. In the mid and late seventies the word transition began to be heard among the people most involved with putting persons with disabilities to work. Soon the transition process would begin placing more and more emphasis in communities and schools to get students with disabilities prepared to work once they left their high school placements. The concept of transition brought to us the idea that training for people with disabilities must begin early in order for the students to learn how to do jobs that had several steps in each of the tasks. It was not until 1991, that some school districts were required to have individualized transition plans for all of the students who had intellectual disabilities.

The concept of transition also brought persons with severe intellectual disabilities additional promise when the concept of supported employment also came into existence. Again the federal government placed monies aside and through demonstration grants and the work of rehabilitation commissions for direct delivery services in the area of supported employment and more funds were allocated for helping the student with the most disabilities to find work. These would include the hard to reach and teach students with autism, severe mental retardation, and cerebral palsy. For the first time these students or the hardest to teach would get a chance to get training in jobs in the community. Since everyone knew it would take longer to train these individuals due to their extreme behaviors nonetheless there was hope for these students. Vocational history had once again been made.

All of these transitions and other major movements such as the vocational Acts amendments, federal monies for transition, and supported employment have brought us closer to serving more and more individuals with severe intellectual disabilities in jobs in the community and thus allowing these students to have more dignity for themselves.

Presently we are in the phase of placing many persons with severe intellectual disabilities in regular education settings. With this emphasis has also come some awareness that there are many children and young adults whose first language is not English. By the year 2000 many minority children will be a majority in our schools and teachers will need information on how to better serve these culturally and linguistically different children who will be in their classrooms.

Thus, vocational education has moved slowly to make jobs and job training a reality for many persons with severe intellectual disabilities but we have just touched the surface for these students. More work remains to be done to finally give more and more students access to jobs, the community, regular classroom instruction, and finally access to some who need instruction in their first language.

ELVA DURÁN, PH.D.

ACKNOWLEDGMENTS

The author wishes to acknowledge so many wonderful people who have helped her see the final end of this book.

Lou Brown, Ph.D., Special Education, University of Wisconsin at Madison, who has always inspired me to continue my work at TASH (The Association for Persons with Severe Handicaps) and has created an awareness for me in providing the best possible education for the student who has severe disabilities.

California State University, Sacramento, Affirmative Action Office, for awarding me $1,300 to have this manuscript typed.

Art and Louie Durán, two of my brothers, who assisted me financially so that I could stay at home during the summer and finish most of my manuscript.

Josephine Durán Lucero, my sister, who encouraged me always to work on this manuscript until I saw the end of the project.

Wen Lee, my former graduate assistant, who assisted me in locating some articles in the library.

Michael John Lewis, Ph.D., my department chair at California State University, Sacramento, for assisting me in discovering ways that I could receive funds to get my manuscript typed. Michael was a wonderful support system.

René Merino, Ph.D., Bilingual Education and Director of the Cross Cultural Resource Center, California State University, Sacramento, who gave me typing support from his Center so that my manuscript could be completed. René thanks for all your support.

Elvia Nava, Terri Wheeler, Arturo Salas, and Lorena Morales of the Cross Cultural Resource Center, California State University, Sacramento, for helping me type this manuscript. They were outstanding and a true team.

Milagros Seda, Ph.D., Associate Professor, Bilingual Education, The University of Texas at El Paso, for providing many materials in the area of bilingual education and English-As-A–Second Language so that I could complete the chapter on Bilingual Methods.

John O. West, Ph.D., English professor at the University of Texas at El Paso, for editing my chapters.

Finally, the Latino parents and so many other parents and their children in El Paso, Texas, who had enough faith in me to have me assist them to find better ways to teach their sons and daughters with autism and other severe disabilities. All of you were my best teachers through the years. I shall not forget you soon.

CONTENTS

VOCATIONAL TRAINING
AND EMPLOYMENT OF THE
MODERATELY AND SEVERELY
HANDICAPPED AND AUTISTIC
ADOLESCENT
WITH PARTICULAR EMPHASIS
TO BILINGUAL
SPECIAL EDUCATION

Chapter One

VOCATIONAL TRAINING

This chapter will explain some different options that can be done in vocational training, and the writer will explain some important types of cuing that is needed in order for students with handicaps to learn to do work. Additionally, how to set up a vocational training program in the community will be explained.

Since the Morrill Act of 1882 (Lynch, 1982) was passed by which land was granted to help vocational education colleges, many changes have taken place which have allowed students with disabilities find work in the community.

BEGINNING A VOCATIONAL PROGRAM

In order to begin any type of vocational training, a good director or teacher who is responsible for teaching students to do various types of work must first see what skills the students presently have. Also the teacher and/or director must further determine the type of students he/she is working with. For example, do the students have severe autism and/or mental retardation, or do the students know and speak only one language? When the students are training on their jobs and know only one language it makes it difficult for them to receive directions in English if no Spanish or home language is used during the training. Questions and considerations such as these will greatly affect how the vocational program will be organized.

CONSIDERING THE TYPES OF STUDENTS
WHO WILL BE PART OF THE TRAINING

This writer has become aware that there are many students, such as those with autism and other severe handicaps, who need to be observed in order to determine if they can stay on task or can attend to any job-related activity. If the student with autism has never worked, then

3

the student will have great difficulty attending or looking at what he/she should be completing. George, a 20 year old student with autism, was first placed in a convalescent center so that he could begin useful work. The college student who was assigned to George and who was acting as vocational trainer or job coach did not realize that George had not been assigned to do vocational tasks prior to his placement in the convalescent center. As a result of this, George started to tantrum and threw dishes and trays on the floor. The trainer attempted to increase George's reinforcers so that he would begin work, but George continued to throw the dishes and trays on the floor. (Reinforcers used with George were things he liked such as decaffeinated coffee and eating raisins.) In ten minutes, George had created such chaos that the trainer did not know what to do. After considerable discussion, the student trainer and the director decided that George had not acquired earlier the skills he needed in order to do the job.

It was decided that George needed to be placed in vocational training that would teach him some skills so that he could work at the convalescent center. A program for teaching George to do simulations of valuable activities was started. Below appears some of the programming which was developed for George.

Day number one: Dishes and a dishwashing bin resembling the materials used to wash dishes at the convalescent center were obtained for George. He was told to wash dishes on command. The trainer stood behind George as he worked and completed his tasks. Each time George completed a task, he was praised and was told he was doing good work. George tantrumed for the entire time (ten minutes) he was trained. A conference was held once again with the director of the project. The college student trainer shared with the director notes he had written concerning George's behavior. After considerable discussion, the director and the college student trainer decided that instead of having George work for ten minutes, his time would be reduced to five minutes. Also, reinforcements would be continued so that George would be given these reinforcements if he worked. Instead of giving George a single reinforcement, he was allowed to choose from a menu of reinforcers. This time, instead of only having George drink decaffeinated coffee, he was allowed to choose from such reinforcers as (1) having George choose from combing his hair, applying cologne, eating some raisins, and eating unsalted pretzels. All of these reinforcers were ones that George really enjoyed. It is important to provide desirable options when setting up reinforcers for students to work or train to do activities. George was also taught to point to whatever pictures he had in his communication booklet.

Day two: George was told to work and this time at the end of every minute George was allowed to choose a reinforcer if he worked on his dishwashing task. George tantrumed and banged his head. When two minutes passed in which he did not engage in these behaviors, George was allowed to choose a reinforcer. Also, as part of George's training he was told to clean, sit down quietly, and listen to a bell that was being played in the background. He was told to do this at least two to three times for five minutes. George was still taught to point to pictures in his communication booklet. George was a non-verbal, mute student.

Day three: George gradually increased his work time to five minutes. His reinforcement schedule was changed to have George work for approximately three minutes before he was allowed to choose his reinforcer. When this time limit was too long for George, he was allowed to choose from reinforcers a minute and a half after he worked correctly on his task. Gradually, on the third day, George tantrumed less and also started to complete more of his task. George was beginning to attend more to assigned tasks. The idea of giving George rewards was helpful in getting him to be more productive on the job training.

Days four and five: George gradually increased his work now to ten minutes, and he did this increase in his time without the need for many reinforcers. By the end of the fifth day, George was working without reinforcers up to thirteen minutes.

When a teacher/program director is certain of the type of students he/she should plan some immediate behavior intervention programming, especially for the students with severe autism and other severe mental retardation. Deciding the type of intervention to use with these students is extremely important, and it must be continued as the programming progresses. Throughout the training period it is helpful in planning what will be done with the students.

This writer has observed in directing a transition program for persons with autism that because of their behaviors, many are difficult to teach. It has further been this writer's experience that many students with autism need to be placed in a compliance training program where they learn to follow directions, such as the Core Management Program developed by Jenson (1984). In Core Management the students learn to follow directions as the first part of the program teaches them to "Get Ready." The teachers will say "Get Ready" on command. The teacher will simultaneously say, "Get Ready" and will have the students place their hands on their laps as the command to "Get Ready" is given. This procedure is usually repeated for about fifteen minutes daily so that the students will begin to learn to follow directions. When the students have learned to follow some directions and are complying with the teacher's command of "Get Ready," they will begin to do other activities that require them to complete their activities.

SETTING UP A VOCATIONAL PROGRAM IN THE COMMUNITY

When attempting to set up a vocational program, it is important to survey the community, a step that is necessary because one must be realistic about what particular jobs are available for the individual. When surveying the community some of the jobs that are available for the students to do are fast food restaurants, clerical, motel service, and having the students work in nursing or convalescent facilities. Once the survey is completed, it is necessary to make an appointment and speak at some length with each of the managers and or directors of the various facilities where possible job sites have been located. When speaking to the managers and or directors of the job sites, the person seeking jobs for the students should inform the people of each of the facilities that someone will need to be supervising the students each time they are training or are working in the various restaurants and other facilities. Also, it is a good idea to give the employers the phone numbers of the people who are responsible for the project and the training that will be done with each student, as well as the phone numbers of each of the job trainers and or coaches. (The teacher or trainer would keep a record for each of the students). For example, each time the student completes his/her command and or task the teacher or trainer completes a plus if the student complied or completed the directions the teacher gave the student.)

The Core Management pattern should be repeated with the student as much as ten to twenty minutes daily, so that management results can be achieved with the students. Without the student's first learning to be compliant, they will not be able to complete various tasks in job training. Further, without the student learning to follow various directions and or commands, the students will not be successful in staying on task for very long periods of time. Compliance training is essential in order for students with severe handicaps to learn to do work and other tasks in the community.

Other types of students who need to be considered when setting up a vocational program in the community are the students who have multiple disabilities. These are students who are brain damaged and may be blind or deaf. Other students who should be considered are students who have epilepsy, may have motor difficulties, or may be in wheelchairs. It is necessary to determine how much disability the students with brain damage and who are blind and or deaf may have, so that appropriate materials can be developed for the students who are learning to do work. For example, if students cannot complete some training, adjustments need to be made so the materials can be highlighted or color coded and enlarged for those students who may have some vision difficulties. If students are required to press buttons on an automatic dishwasher, for instance, the trainer will need to color one of the buttons of the dishwasher so that the student will know which is the "on" and is "off." Also if students have epilepsy, for example, it will be important for the trainers to place those students who could possibly have a gran mal seizure in a job where they will not hurt themselves. There should be no sharp objects or other types of objects which could hurt them. It is important to assess the working environments carefully. Much time can be saved if students are appropriately placed in a work environment which will not cause them physical harm.

Another type of student whose work environment must be carefully assessed is the student who is a drooler. Droolers need to be placed in their working areas where they are not going to drop their saliva on the food or water they are handling. A drooler needs to be constantly reminded to keep his/her head back and to close the lips while training and working on a particular task. Job managers will often cause a student to reject their work if students drool on the work they are completing.

If a problem arises on the job while the student with disabilities is working, the manager/directors of the facilities will know they can reach the person. For students with severe behaviors, for example, students with autism, it is always helpful for employers to realize they can call someone if severe problems arise with the students they have in training, and who are working in their facilities.

It has been the experience of this writer that when several students with autism were placed in various job sites and they refused to work or exhibited unusual behaviors, it was always a very good thing for the directors to know they could call either the job coach and or the director of the vocational program and seek help in problems that might be arising from having the student on a particular job. If the people on the job sites do not feel like they have enough support, they may not be open to allowing students with disabilities to do work in their facilities. The amount of support given to managers etc. is critical in terms of having future students work in the various sites.

Especially autistic students must be carefully considered when beginning a vocational training program. Students with autism have, in this writer's opinion, been the most challenging to place and train in jobs in the community. Part of the difficulty with placing these students is that they are very unpredictable in their behavior; thus, more precautions have to be taken with these students. For example, since students with autism experience preservation of sameness Lovaas (1977) (with preservation of sameness the students with autism do not want their environments changed in any form or in any part or detail). If change occurs the students with autism become extremely angry and tantrum. It is important to introduce these students gradually into new situations where they are among other people. When one begins training these students early when they are twelve or thirteen years old they become more and more accustomed to being among other people in public. This is one of the approaches which works the best with these students. They need programming beginning early in their lives, and they also need to be exposed to change gradually instead of trying to do all of it at once. It generally takes years to teach students with autism how to be among others in work and in the community.

As already described earlier in this chapter, another factor will greatly affect the progress made by students with autism attempting on-the-job training is successful compliance training.

Additionally, when beginning a program in vocational skills training, it is important to hold a training session or workshop for the co-workers and job managers to be involved, so they can be informed concerning the types of students with disabilities who are going to be in training. In the workshop the co-workers need to be enlightened concerning the various disabilities they may face with the students. All should be explained to the co-workers and job managers, in simple and comprehensible terms, so there will not be any confusion nor lack of understanding concerning the students with disabilities. Some topics that might be included in preparing for a workshop for co-workers and job managers appear below:

FIGURE 1
Workshop Outline for Employers and Co-Workers

1. Define the various disabilities.

2. Show slides of students working.

3. Talk about the student's behavior difficulties.

4. Explain and demonstrate some management procedures that can be used with students involved in the programming.

5. Talk about the length of training and placing students on-the-job training.

6. Discuss superstitions that may affect some of the co-workers and employment while on-the-job training.

7. Questions and answers.

This writer noted in directing her vocational project in the Southwest that many co-workers and employers accepted students with disabilities more readily when the co-workers and employers understood their particular disabilities. This was especially true of many of the older Latino co-workers in one particular setting where students with disabilities were placed to do work. The older and more set in their ways and culture the co-workers were, the harder it was for them to accept anyone else in their particular job sites, especially if the disabilities involved were not understood.

Besides giving co-workers and employers an orientation workshop, parents, teachers, and administrators also need to be informed about the vocational programming which is going to take place. For too many of the parents, especially Latino parents, having their children learn academics is of first importance. They measure their children's success by what their children know in terms of mathematics, reading, and writing. In a questionnaire given to over 150 Latino parents from the Southwest, many of them noted that what was important for the sons or daughters to learn was how to read, write, and spell. Since they viewed work as not being very important for their son or daughter to do, a training workshop informing the parents, teachers, and administrators of the vocational programming is important in order for all concerned to become more supportive of their sons or daughters and their working on the job. It takes constant working with parents to help them see the value of allowing their sons or daughters to work in the community.

Every six months to a year, some type of questionnaire needs to be sent to the parents in order to ascertain how they feel about the vocational training their students are participating in. One that was developed by this writer and was sent to 150 Latino parents in the Southwest appears below:

FIGURE 2

Questionnaire Developed in Order to Determine How Parents Felt
About the Vocational Progress Their Sons and or Daughters Participated In.

Inventario Para Los Padres y Madres

1. What is Vocational Training?
   ¿Qué es entrenamiento vocacional?

2. Do you want your son and or daughter to work once school has been completed?
   ¿Desea que su hijo o hija trabaje cuando termine sus estudios?

3. Do you want your son and or daughter to earn money?
   ¿Quiere que su hijo o hija reciba dinero por su trabajo?

4. What is transition?
   ¿Qué es transición?

When the questionnaire was analyzed, it was discovered that over half of the parents did not know why their sons and daughters were working. Also, many parents felt that they would live forever and therefore did not feel their students should work. Three-fourths of the parents noted that they did not know what the terms "transition" and "vocational training" meant.

After such information was revealed, another more intense workshop was given to parents so they could better understand what they did not know as indicated by the questionnaire. Every month teachers and instructional aides involved with the vocational training would call parents to see if any problem was occurring. This helped bring any problem to light immediately.

The constant communication that must be carried forth in working with the community should not be taken lightly nor should it be overlooked.

VOCATIONAL TRAINING:
TECHNIQUES FOR JOB COACHES AND TRAINERS

A major part of successful vocational training is knowing how to train students to learn to do various types of jobs and work in the community Brown, (1989); Wehman (1980,81); Bellamy, (1987).

Some of the techniques which make for effective job coach training were developed by Marc Gold (1980), a pioneer in the field of vocational skill training who believed strongly that persons with severe disabilities could be trained to do work. Prior to this, many people did not believe such students could do anything useful.

Verbal Cuing. One technique that is especially useful is verbal cuing. With verbal cuing, the trainer gives short, brisk directions to the student. For example, the trainer will say "Press *on.*" This indicates that the student is to press the "on" button of a particular machine. In this case the machine may be an automatic dishwasher.

When giving verbal cues, the cues should be short and brisk to prevent a student with severe disabilities from becoming confused. Too often, if the cues are too long the student will fail to follow directions. Gold (1980) noted that the shorter the cuing is for the student, the more easily the student responds to directions. Gold further noted that instead of telling students they had made an error on a particular task, that it was important to suggest that they "Try another way." The words "Try another way" are a signal for the student that he/she had made an error and needed to find another way to do the particular task.

Verbal cuing should be phased out as the student learns to do the job more effectively. Verbal cuing should also be done as unobtrusively as possible, so that coworkers in the workplace will not become too aware of the student who is involved in training on-the-job. If the student is of another language or speaks another language than English, it is important to cue the student initially in the student's dominant or home language. As the student becomes more accustomed to hearing the second language the directions can then be given in English, and the student's home language can be used briefly at the beginning to make sure the student has understood what needs to be done when the commands are given in English.

Physical Guidance. Physical guidance when used as cuing should be done so that the co-worker knows what he/she is doing incorrectly. In physical guidance the trainer or job coach will place the hands over the student's hands. As the trainer places the hands over the student's hands, the trainer models so that the student knows how to do a particular step or job correctly.

For example, the student may be wiping tables incorrectly, if the student has not learned this task correctly from the beginning. The trainer carefully places a hand over the student's hand and shows the student the particular motions to be used in wiping the table correctly. The job coach should not remove his/her hands from the student's hands until the student has correctly practiced the particular motions he/she is to complete.

Gesturing. Gesturing is another type of cuing which is used in special education training. In gesturing, the trainer or job coach will point to the area or place where the student is to make the correction. Also in gesturing, the job coach may use hand motion so that the student knows how to complete or redo the particular task or step for the task.

Modeling. When modeling is used, the trainer or job coach completes one or two steps and the student does the steps that were shown to him/her to complete. The job coach or trainer continues this process until each step has been modeled for the student. The student then completes each step.

This writer has not found this type of cuing effective with severely handicapped and autistic students. Part of the difficulty in modeling not being effective with persons with severe handicaps is that the students often cannot keep focused on what they are doing because of their extreme behavior difficulties or lack of attending behaviors. As a result they sometimes fail to learn even one step that is shown or modeled to them.

Demonstration. In demonstration, all of the steps of a particular task are shown to the student all at once. The job coach takes time to make certain that the student has learned what to do, repeating the demonstration if needed. Once again, this writer has not found the demonstration technique to be effective when used with severely handicapped autistic students. As with modeling, these students have great attending problems and are not able to sit quietly or look as the job coach shows them what to do. For more moderately disabled or higher functioning students, this type of cuing can be effective.

Combination of Some Cuing Techniques. It is effective to use some of the above types of cuing together. For example, using verbal and physical guidance cuing can be effective. Gesturing when used together with verbal cuing and physical guidance can also be effective.

This writer has used several techniques together or in combination when she and her job coaches have trained students with autism and other severe handicaps to do the work. Best results have been obtained when using verbal cuing and physical guidance. Students with autism respond to verbal cuing and some gesturing and physical guidance. It is worth noting that if the physical guidance cues have not been used with students with autism gradually, then the student may not be willing to have a job coach or trainer place his/her hands over the hands of a particular student. The key is using many of these cuing techniques a little at a time and consistently. Eventually, the cuing techniques can be phased out as the student learns to work more independently on the job.

UTILIZING COLLEGE STUDENTS AND COMMUNITY PERSONS TO DO THE JOB COACHING AND TRAINING OF STUDENTS WITH DISABILITIES

Wehman (1980) and Brown (1989, 1991) have often spoken about the successes that can be reached if students from a nearby university or people in the community can be utilized to assist with the training of students to find jobs in the community.

As this writer discovered in various cities in Texas, one of the concerns that continually arose was that people in the community wanted to know how they could get help to train and to place students in the community. Many public school personnel and staff did not know exactly how to get universities to help them. A few of them felt that there was a large gap between the universities and the community.

The writer's suggestion each time was for the public schools or someone within the schools to contact a particular person within a department to see who could help people set up vocational programming in the community. (If a university person is available to assist public school personnel in helping with training students who have disabilities, university people may need to assist students in finding training sites and jobs, so that the public schools will have a better opportunity to succeed with the students).

Brown (1990) notes that working closely with university professors or university personnel can make it possible for college students to work with the students with disabilities. The ratio of staff per student with disabilities is greatly enhanced with the help of university students acting as trainers for the students or clients.

This writer started a very successful community-based vocational program in the Southwest utilizing her college students who were enrolled in a vocational class in special education. First she made certain the students knew how to do the various types of cuing to assist the clients as they learned how to do the various types of training, utilizing training techniques already explained earlier in this chapter. In order to make certain that the college students had learned the techniques, this writer observed each college student to see if they could do the various types of techniques. She had the students do simulations, so that they could demonstrate how the techniques would be accomplished in the field. The simulations were then accomplished in various vocational training sites. The college students personally completed each job for the first time, so they could teach the clients how to do each job with each step involved.

After the college students practiced each job, they proceeded to write each step of the job on a task analysis sheet. Task analysis sheets (Gold, 1980) are an excellent means of determining if the student can complete each step of the job he/she is preparing to do and complete. Figure 3 shows how each step of the task is delineated on each line of the task analysis. Across each line where steps of the job have been designated, the trainer marks with a slash mark each area or step where the student/client needs improvement. The steps are left blank wherever the student does not need assistance.

Upon completing the task, the trainer would look at the task analysis and would note how many steps have been left without slash marks. The steps without slash marks indicate the independent performance of the student. For example, if the student had ten steps to do and accomplished only five of them, the student would get fifty percent correct of the steps involved or would be independent approximately fifty percent of the time on this task. Thus, the college students acting as trainers do the various tasks, then practice coding as if they were teaching the students to do the tasks. Obviously, it is important for college students or persons practicing the various vocational tasks to also practice coding the students to do work. This writer has found that the more simulated practice the college students do, the more smoothly the various training is accomplished once actual training and programming begin.

Following the coding on the task analysis, the college students trade places with other students so they can practice doing other vocational jobs. Such practice again allows each student to learn not only his/her job but a second job. This experience assures that the college student can train and place a variety of students once the actual training begins.

Parents of the children are also brought to the vocational simulations to learn how to do the different jobs their children will be learning to do.

FIGURE 3

Task Analysis of Students Washing Dishes on Automatic Dishwasher

	Student: Task: Date:					
10. *Begin with #1 again*	10	10	10	10	10	10
9. *Stack dishes in appropriate stacks*	9	9	9	9	9	9
8. *Sort dishes*	8	8	8	8	8	8
7. *Collect dishes at other end*	7	7	7	7	7	7
6. *Check to see dishes are facing downwards*	6	6	6	6	6	6
5. *Press on button*	5	5	5	5	5	5
4. *Place dishes on rack*	4	4	4	4	4	4
3. *Clean dishes with cloth*	3	3	3	3	3	3
2. *Add soap to bin of water*	2	2	2	2	2	2
1. *Place dishes on bin*	1	1	1	1	1	1

DATE: December 15, 1991

50% independence on task. Student needed assistance on 5 steps of task.

The steps are marked 1–10 in the order that the job is performed. The trainer puts a slash (/) mark beside any step in the task where the student needed any kind of assistance (verbal or physical guidance) to do that particular step or steps. In this particular diagram the student needed assistance to perform steps #1, #3, #6, #8, and #9. Slash marks were placed beside these particular numbers above. There were five other numbers that did not have slash marks and that is considered this particular student's independence performance. Thus the student obtained 50% independence on the task.

Parents often become excellent volunteers. Many are happy to assist in the programming, but generally they need training and guidance in order to learn how to do the various tasks and programming that their children will be learning to complete. When parents become involved from the beginning of the process, they have a strong tendency to remain part of the program throughout the program's operation. If parents speak another language or are from a different culture, every effort should be made to teach the parents in their own language. This procedure is critically important so the parents can feel they are a part of the programming.

In a study this writer completed in the Southwest (1991), she learned that many culturally and linguistically different parents of Mexican and Mexican American families felt left out because training that was made often failed to use the parent's home or primary language. Parents noted they felt lost and did not know various terms, simply because they did not understand English, the language in which these terms were communicated to them.

Following the simulated training of the college students and parents, the college students and the other volunteers should be shown slides of the students/clients they will be training in the vocational program. This procedure helps the volunteers and trainers see the type of students they will be working with directly. As the slides of the different clients/students are shown, various characteristics of the students should be pointed out so that trainers will have an idea of the cognitive abilities of each student and the type of management that will be needed. A positive comment should be made on each student so that the trainers will begin to look forward to the first day of training. One example of a positive comment that could be made would be to say, for instance, "María works as hard as she can, considering her off task behavior at times. She can now complete her job in half the time it took her to do it at the beginning of the programming."

The college students and or volunteers should also be given clear understanding of the seriousness of what they are about to begin as they start the programming. They need to realize that persons with disabilities have already lost much time, and if the trainers do not stimulate the students to work hard, the students will not make the progress they should. The trainers should be assured from the beginning that they will receive some correction feedback in order to help them learn the techniques even faster. If college students realize they will be given feedback, they will expect this and not feel threatened when the training begins and the supervisors begin telling them how they could possibly improve. (Written reports give the trainer a better chance to correct any problems).

Often it is not possible to talk to each student trainer while the training is taking place; thus, it is a good idea to write on an observation and feedback sheet how the student could possibly improve. In her own training, this writer has developed and used a sheet that she uses to give correction-feedback to students. Figure 4 gives an example of the form and Figure 5 gives an example of how the feedback is given to students.

College students have indicated that having an evaluation done on them helps them usually see how they can improve, and gives them a record for future comparison as they improve. The supervisor who is evaluating the students will be more likely to complete evaluation on the trainer if a form is available that needs to be completed on the person doing the training.

FIGURE 4

Name of Student: **Name of Supervisor:**
School or Training Site:
Date:

Strengths of Student:

Areas for Improvements:

Signature: _____ I have seen this sheet.

Signature: _____ I have not seen this sheet.

FIGURE 5

Name of Student: Bettie   **Name of Supervisor:** Durán
School or Training Site: Community
Date: December 10, 1990

Strengths of Student:
      You gave excellent verbal cuing to the student as he was working on the job. Your coding sheet was also nicely done. You used excellent vocational training techniques. You stood behind your client and this helped your client reach independence.

Areas for Improvements:
      Evaluate consistently throughout the hour training session. Have the student return all of his materials he used in training back to original area.

Signature: _____ I have seen this sheet.

Signature: _____ I have not seen this sheet.

After college students or volunteers have been trained, it is important to note how many college students or trainers will be working with each of the clients or students of the program, since, as Brown (1990) notes, a ratio of one trainer or adult per client is ideal, but a ratio of one adult per two students with severe disabilities is also acceptable. In coordinating several vocational training programs, this writer has found that if a supervisor or trainer puts two students with extreme behavior and or severe conditions together, it will be difficult to give appropriate cuing to the students, due to their severe conditions. If one student with moderate disabilities is paired along with a student of more severe disabilities, then the supervision will be easier on the trainer. Also, the training will be more effective because one student will not be receiving all of the attention due to the severity of his/her condition.

Locating vocational training sites in the community is also another necessary step in establishing a vocational training program.

This writer has taken much time to search throughout the community for different places where students with disabilities can be trained. Such a search takes much leg work because often managers of various fast food restaurants, for example, do not fully understand vocational training programming, and need to have face-to-face contact with persons who are attempting to find training sites and employment for persons who have disabilities. If persons with disabilities have not been seen in various job sites in the communities, then it will become necessary to speak personally to many managers and personnel directors.

The importance of face-to-face contact cannot be underestimated. This writer has found several more jobs sites for training by using the personal approach than by calling managers over the phone. The biggest drawback of this personal approach is that it takes much time to go from employer to employer. This writer has also trained college students and gone with them after their training to make certain they have learned the most important points to explain to employers.

By training other people to assist in the vocational programming, more sites can be located for the clients and or students. Because this writer was working in a primarily Spanish-speaking community, it was necessary that persons assisting in finding training sites for the clients be able to speak Spanish.

Many of the employers or managers may know only one language, or feel most comfortable speaking in a dominant language; rapport can more easily be established if the employer's and/or manager's language is also spoken by the project persons.

In many Mexican American communities, a sense of trust must be developed before some employers and or managers and community people can allow other persons to become part of their immediate group or work site.

LOCATING VOCATIONAL TRAINING SITES IN THE COMMUNITY

Locating vocational training sites in the community is also another necessary step in establishing a vocational program.

This process could take anywhere from a month to a year. A good training program always has staff looking for jobs for those who are at home and are not employed. The best vocational training programs are seen where the staff of the program goes out at least twice weekly from morning until afternoon to find jobs for the clients of the program.

Through the years this writer has learned many things which are helpful when going to the community to find jobs for the clients of one's program. Some of the ideas are listed below:

1) Employers need to see a written prospectus which explains the purpose of the vocational program, how many students are involved in the training, and who are the staff responsible for the clients/students once they are placed in the program.

2) Most employees respond more favorably if staff members approaching them and are professionaly dressed. Employers have a tendency to be more receptive to people who come through their doors if they appear neat and are professionally dressed.

3) Employers also want to know what other students have been successfully placed in training programs.

4) Employers want to know the amount of time required for their personnel, as well as the names and phone numbers of various staff members and how to reach them in case of an emergency.

5) Employers want to know about the various disabling conditions of the students so they can best understand who will be working in their work areas and job sites.

6) Employers want to know about any particular behavior problems

the students may have which may prevent them from working to the fullest.

7) Employers appreciate staff who follow up the progress of students and check at the job sites to make certain there are no major problems with various students as the training progresses.

Once the basic information sheets for each client are completed, and similar information gathered for each prospective employment site, then comes a period during which a client and the job training site can be matched for the best results.

Every community is different, and where one type of job may be a good one for one community for employing people with disabilities, in another community this particular job may not be the best.

In the community where this writer directed the adult transition project, fast food restaurants seemed to be the main place where jobs could be found for students with disabilities. This writer often was told by several job managers that few people ever wanted to work the very early job shifts, for example from 7:00 a.m. until 10:00 a.m.. During this particular time, many fast food restaurants want employees who will shred lettuce, slice pickles and tomatoes and otherwise prepare for the rush noon hour where customers buy a large quantity of hamburgers or sandwiches. Also, employers of fast food restaurants often want employees to help prepare other foods, such as the dough pastries which are fried and sold as desserts during the noon and dinner hour.

According to employers, few college students or other prospective employees want to work the early morning shifts at fast food restaurants. This makes many jobs available for clients who need jobs once they have been trained for them.

For another example, travel agencies often need employees who can sort travel catalogs for customers who are going to travel to different countries or places, or the employee will be needed to stamp each catalog that the travel agency receives with an address label of the travel agency. This writer has placed several students in various travel agencies, to perform such tasks as sorting and arranging catalogues as they arrive. In other cases, the travel agency needed clients to clean the restrooms by sweeping and mopping, and perform other simple tasks.

Small travel agencies, for instance, are more open to hiring students with disabilities than are larger travel agencies, because smaller agency's staff is small and someone is needed to take care of the catalogues and other travel materials. Employees who work in the travel agency often do not have time to do janitorial work or have time to sort and arrange travel catalogues. These types of jobs are ideal for persons with disabilities.

Additionally, universities make for excellent training sites for students with disabilities. Later, when success with training has been achieved, many of these sites become potentials for hiring people with disabilities. Some of the types of jobs this writer has found for students with disabilities at a university site have been stuffing envelopes and stamping address information at an alumni office where mail goes out constantly, requesting ex-students who have been graduated from the university to donate money to various programs.

Other jobs which are available are those in food service. At the university where this particular project was coordinated, the union cafeteria offered busing of tables, cleaning of table tops with water and chlorine bleach, and sweeping areas where carts were moved around as tables were cleaned of dishes and other food trays, etc..

In the kitchen area of the university union clients loaded or unloaded automatic dish washers and arranged dishes on shelves for future use.

Other jobs in food service included washing, drying, and wrapping potatoes in foil so they were a popular item among university folk and once again students/clients did an excellent job preparing potatoes for the lunch hour.

The food service manager was so pleased with all that the clients were accomplishing in his facility that he toured the food service area and came up with other ideas and job possibilities which could be completed by the clients. As time went on, the food manager hired two of the clients full time because he was so pleased with their progress.

In addition general skills in janitorial work in the food service area were found to be useful elsewhere. For example, many of the clients learned to mop and vacuum using the equipment provided by the food service department or the janitorial service itself.

Additional jobs that were found for the students were in a convalescent home. The convalescent home was situated near the university and was within walking distance of the other jobs that were around the university cafeteria and alumni office. In the convalescent center there were several food service jobs and folding of linens that could be accomplished by the clients. One job in particular that many students enjoyed doing was filling glasses with water and fruit juice for the elderly patients who were in the convalescent home. The patients enjoyed young people coming to them with fruit juices and water, and the clients enjoyed being useful to the elderly.

In the convalescent center, once again, two of the students were hired permanently. The director of the center was very happy with the way the clients treated the old people. Also the director believed that the elderly in the home were very happy when the clients were around them.

The types of jobs around each community vary. If one begins to search for the different possibilities, then one is usually surprised to find so many possibilities throughout the community. When one job is found, then pretty soon another job possibility can be found as the good word spreads about what students are doing at different sites.

It takes much hard work and patience to locate jobs in different communities. Above all it takes a great amount of persistence, because many employers have never had people with disabilities work for them, and they may not understand how valuable clients can be until they have hired some of them.

PROVIDING FOLLOW-UP AND SUPPORT TO EMPLOYERS, CLIENTS AND PARENTS

Probably one of the most important components in vocational training and permanent employment for students with disabilities is assuring that adequate follow-up occurs. Another important component of vocational training is noting if appropriate support is given to the clients and to the employers who hire these different clients.

By visiting the job sites weekly at the beginning, the supervisory staff begins to let employers realize that the staff members care about the students who have been placed to work in the different worksites. If there are problems initially or as time progresses, the staff will become aware promptly if there is a difficulty with the clients or other co-workers involved in on-the-job training. Some of the follow-up may include a talk with the clients so they can know that they are doing good work or if they need to work harder.

Students with autism, for example, often do not recall what they may have done which was inappropriate, but with a short conversation from staff members, the student can recall his/her behavior and improve it if it was not appropriate. Further offering follow-up to the student can include showing the student a progress chart of the work that has been performed or not performed, so the student can continue improving or working harder.

As the student improves, the amount of follow-up and observations can be reduced to eventually occur only once a month to every three months. By following the various procedures which have been mentioned, supervisors can monitor student progress carefully so that the student succeeds in the job he/she is attempting to learn.

In the project that this writer coordinated, it was often helpful to encourage the clients and let them know that they were doing well on the job. Students with autism became frustrated, and explaining to them what they were doing well or were improving in was helpful to the amount of progress the students would accomplish.

Employers and parents also need the support of the staff. Many an employer is not aware that clients often could do better if they were encouraged more. It is necessary to instruct the employers, giving them information on how clients learn best. Many employers are often encouraged to provide support to clients once they realize that providing words of positive encouragement can improve the client's level of productivity.

Parents of disabled students often feel discouraged because they are not able to determine if their son and or daughter will stay on the job. Many lose perspective because they do not see long term results and are too often limited to experiencing the worst situations of their sons and daughters. Caregivers who work closely with parents of disabled students must often help them see the progress that is being made by their son and or daughter. Also, when the sons or daughters are not doing well at their jobs it is important to encourage parents and offer positive support. How one works with parents during parents' difficult periods can mean the difference of whether parents remain supportive of their son and or daughter through the entire vocational training and possible later employment.

This writer has learned through the years that parents are a crucial part of the child's success or failure with on-the-job training. Giving parents the extra time and support they need will help with the long process which is ahead in getting their help in keeping their son and or daughter progressing on-the-job.

As director of the adult program, this writer learned the value of working closely with parents through the years. Parents often have many worries and are deeply troubled about their sons or daughters especially if there has been a history of their not doing well on different programs or job training. One useful technique is to invite parents to come to the job site and see that their son or daughter is doing well on the particular job he/she is training on or is working at. Sometimes even calling parents on the telephone can be a big help to them, and they feel that someone cares about them. Many parents often need someone to listen to them as they share their doubts, fears, and concerns of their son or daughter being able to find or do work.

Through the years, this writer came to know several parents and somehow their concerns became concerns of this writer. Parents often do not have someone close to share their doubts and fears, especially someone who is knowledgeable about their situation. By giving parents a little time they can be assisted to better understand their feelings and can be helped to feel supported with their son or daughter as he/she begins to work.

Vocational training includes many components, such as finding the jobs, getting the clients and trainers prepared to do the different work, and offering support and follow-up to employers, clients and parents. The success of this major component cannot be overlooked, because little can be accomplished with the person with disabilities without the vocational training component.

REFERENCES

Bellamy, T. G., et al. (1987). *Supported Employment: A Community Implementation Guide.* Baltimore: Paul Brookes.

Brown, L. (1989). "A Strategy for Evaluating the Vocational Milieu of a Worker with Severe Intellectual Disabilities" Version IV, University of Wisconsin and Madison Metropolitan School District, pp. 1–21.

Brown, L. (1990). "Integration of Students with Severe Disabilities," Tash Annual Conference, Chicago, Illinois.

Brown, L. (1991). How much time should students with severe intellectual disabilities spend in regular education classrooms and elsewhere? *JASH*, Vol. 16, No I. pp. 39–47.

Durán, E. (1991). Effects of Using Spanish only, Spanish and English, and English only cues with students of limited English proficiency who have moderate to severe disabilities, *OSERS News & Print, Disability and People from Minority Background* Vol. III, No. 4, pp. 24–27.

Gold, M. (1980). *More Gold: Did I Say That? Articles and Commentary on the Try Another Way System.* Champaign, IL: Research Press.

Gold, M. (1980). *Try Another Way Training Manual.* Champaign, IL: Research Press.

Jenson, W. (1984). Workshop entitled, "Compliance training for persons with severe autism," College of Education, The University of Texas at El Paso.

Lovaas, I. (1977). *The Autistic Child Language Development Through Behavior Modification:* Irvington, pp. 18–29.

Lynch, K. P. et al. (1982). *Prevocational and Vocational Education for Special Needs Youth: A Blueprint for the 1980's.* Baltimore: Paul Brookes, pp. 3–33.

Wehman, P. (1981). *Competitive Employment: New Horizons for Severely Disabled Individuals.* Baltimore: Paul Brookes.

Wehman, P. (1980). *Vocational Curriculum for Developmentally Disabled Persons.* Baltimore: Paul Brookes.

Chapter Two

SUPPORTED EMPLOYMENT

Supported employment is a relatively new concept in vocational education. It is an initiative that is designed to provide persons with severe disabilities on-going support so that eventually the clients/students can stay at work at least twenty hours monthly and get minimum or somewhat below minimum wage. This chapter will give the federal definition of supported employment and will explain some of the regulations which make up supported employment. Also this chapter will note some of the different work options that can be utilized to help clients qualify for this opportunity to work at meaningful employment.

Further, this chapter will explain how to set up a supported employment program, utilizing university college students as trainers. Agreements between the employee and the people who have placed the student/client in training will also be noted in this chapter. The individualized habilitation plan designed to set the goals for the student will further be explained. Some advantages and disadvantages of using this model for persons with severe disabilities will also be noted.

Finally, this chapter will note actual experiences and examples of using this model based on programming that has been developed utilizing the supported employment concept. Agreements of individualized habilitation plans will be provided also in Spanish to assist parents and/or care providers who teach and work with the student of limited English proficiency.

WHAT IS SUPPORTED EMPLOYMENT?

As stated earlier in this chapter, supported employment is a very new concept in the vocational education literature. It was developed and federal money was set aside for supported employment because for too long students with mild disabilities were the students who were placed to work in competitive employment. The Rehabilitation Act of 1973 and P.L. 94-142 the Education for All Handicapped Children Act of 1975

27

(Fredricks, 1987) mandate equal educational opportunities for students with handicaps. These Acts are landmark legislation that helped to establish the concept of supported employment. Another Act which gave great impetus to the creation of the supported employment concept was the Carl D. Perkins Vocational Education Act (P.L. 98-524). In this Act, funding was provided for handicapped, disadvantaged individuals and adults who are in need of training.

Supported Employment is defined according to the Texas Rehabilitation Commission (1989) as competitive work in an integrated work setting with on-going support services for individuals with severe handicaps. Competitive employment has either not occurred, or has been interrupted or intermittent as a result of severe handicaps for these individuals. This definition of supported employment includes transitional employment for individuals with chronic mental illness.

The Federal Register (1987) defines Supported Employment to mean competitive work in an integrated work setting for individuals who, because of their handicaps, need on-going support services to perform that work.

Some of these features characterize Supported Employment: (1) people who have severe handicaps who require immediate long term support if employment is to occur and continue with these students; (2) paid, competitive employment for at least 20 hours per week; (3) opportunity for interaction with non-disabled people at the worksite; (4) on-going support to assist in job retention (Texas Rehabilitation, 1989).

Another important feature that characterizes Supported Employment is that whenever the students are placed to work, the setting must be integrated or must have people employed in the area who are without disabilities or who perform regularly in the community. This particular characteristic is crucial to the definition, in that people with disabilities often learn to pattern after other employees; thus, if they have people without disabilities to pattern after, they also learn and model appropriate behaviors.

Some of the disability groups that fall under the term *severe* are the following: the student with autism, the student who has mental retardation, the student with cerebral palsy, mental illness, or other multiple disabilities. These particular groups of students were often the groups of students who never got jobs in the area of vocational education before the advent of supported employment.

REFERRALS TO SUPPORTED EMPLOYMENT

A referral is a person with severe handicaps who is seeking competitive employment, and who will need on-going support services in order to perform competitive work. These referrals for the supported employment services can come from a variety of sources. Some of the sources include (1) the secondary schools; (2) adult day programs; (3) self referrals such as those made from parents, guardians, and interested others, (4) sheltered workshops; and (5) work activity centers.

It has been the experience of this writer that many programs which are utilizing Supported Employment funds are not truly placing in their programs the students/clients who are truly severely handicapped and/or do truly come from the categories noted above. This writer has noted that many of the students/clients who are utilizing Supported Employment funds in different parts of the community are far less severe in their disabilities than what the definition ever intended. The fault for this situation falls directly upon programs and funding agencies who do not screen the clients/students carefully and who place in their programs only those students who are more mildly impaired because these are the easiest to train and place on jobs.

At the University of Texas at El Paso, this writer directed an adult transition program, and three adults with autism were placed in jobs utilizing supported employment funds. In two cases the students with autism were trained to the point that they could handle their jobs at fast food restaurants in four months. In the other case the student with autism was trained to do her job, also at a fast food restaurant, in five months. In each of these cases the students had autism and had intelligence quotients ranging from 12 to 20. Also, each of the students had some compliance problems and was mentally retarded. It is important to note that the clients/students who were placed in jobs in this particular autism project had received early vocational training through the public schools in the community. The clients had started their training when they were twelve and thirteen years old. This writer believes that in order for supported employment to be effective with more severe groups, the student's vocational training must begin as early as eleven and or twelve years of age. It takes longer and requires a greater amount of time to place difficult-to-teach students in community based settings. It takes longer to place students/clients with autism on jobs in the community than any other group of students with other severe handicaps.

SOME EVALUATION CRITERIA
AND STUDENT ELIGIBILITY
FOR SUPPORTED EMPLOYMENT

Handicapped students are often referred to school counselors or others who are charged with overseeing such students, in order to determine their qualifications for supported employment funds. In their vocational evaluation the students are tested to see if they can stay on task and perform basic academic skills. Evaluations of the students/clients are paid for using funds which are designated as supported employment funds. Usually no more than four assessments will be paid for a client or student who has been referred for vocational assessment. A medical examination is also required of the student who is attempting to qualify for supported employment funds.

Once all of the evaluative tests are completed on the student, the following criteria are used to establish if the client/student is eligible for supported employment services:

(1) The applicant has such severe handicaps that he/she will need on-going support services to keep a job, after the case is closed.

(2) The applicant can benefit from placement and training in a competitive employment setting, working with and around nondisabled people.

(3) A public or private, non-profit organization or other resource has agreed to make a written commitment to provide the on-going support services, after the case is closed, for the duration of the employment. (Texas Rehabilitation Commission, 1989).

Additionally, the vocational counselor must document in the case record the factors considered in establishing the individual's eligibility. Documentation is in the form of a continuing contact report that contains certification of the following elements: that the individual

(1) has severe handicaps and requires on-going support services in order to work,

(2) has been determined by an evaluation of rehabilitation potential to have the ability or potential to engage in an on-the-job training program, and

(3) has the ability or can learn to work in a competitive work setting with non-disabled people.

(Texas Rehabilitation Commission, 1989)

SERVICES PROVIDED BY SUPPORTED EMPLOYMENT

The counselor can request additional services under the Supported Employment funds, some of which are

(1) Evaluation of the rehabilitation potential for supported employment which is supplementary to an evaluation initiated using regular case service funds
(2) Development of and placement in jobs
(3) provision of training and/or traditionally time-limited, post employment services which are purchased from a public or private organization or other resources that are needed to support the trainers in employment, such as
   a. intensive on-the-job training and other training provided by skilled job trainees;
   b. provision of follow-up services, including regular contact with employers, trainees with severe handicaps, parents, guardians or other representatives or trainees in order to reinforce and stabilize the job placement;
   c. regular observation or supervision of individuals with severe handicaps at the work site.

An additional service that can be paid for with supported employment funds (up to $20 per hour) if needed to support and assist an individual in entering and succeeding in the program, is

Consumer and Family Orientation. This service involves explaining and gaining support of the client and family members about supported employment the possible impact on benefits, transportation arrangements, client safety, ways and benefits derived from the job, the specific responsibilities of the service provided, the client and family members in making the supported employment placement successful. The maximum number of hours the Commission can pay for this service is 5 hours. (Texas Rehabilitation Commission, 1989).

It has been observed that often parents do not understand why their son or daughter should work or should even leave the home of the parent. This provision makes available money to help explain to parents and clients the importance of supported employment, assistance which is extremely helpful to the job coach or rehabilitation counselor, who has to spend less time trying to explain to the parents of clients how important it is that their son or daughter work in the community. Frequently much time is spent initially helping parents understand the importance of their son's or daughter's working and becoming a contributing member of the work force. The orientation service will help smooth the way for better parent and client acceptance, and may even involve showing them various worksites in the community, thus helping the parents support their son or daughter as actual work begins.

Many Latino parents especially become extremely protective and often do not want their son or daughter to leave the house, because many feel their son or daughter will not need to work. This writer has worked especially hard explaining to many Latino parents who have students with autism that they must let their son or daughter try to work at a particular job. This counseling procedure with the parents often takes more than the five hours provided for by the TRC, but a large portion of the counseling with the parents can be accomplished during that time.

Another service provided in supported employment involves evaluation of the individual's actual performance on the job. After the potential for a work assignment has been made, it is vital to follow it up with actual observation, since *potential* is not always found to be successful. Often more than one job placement must be tried before a successful supported employment can be achieved.

It has been my experience that this service is highly important because too often clients/students are evaluated with various screening devices and this is not what is helpful to the client. A paper and pencil type test does not measure the student's/clients' actual work potential. This writer has observed this especially with students/clients with autism. Autistic students may be unpredictable in behavior while being tested and may not show good results. If these same students are not observed in a work situation, then the students' real work potential cannot be properly assessed. It is highly important that a client's work ability and time on the job be observed so that various people who are not familiar with the client/student can see what he/she can actually do.

One particular student who was referred for supported employment services to a rehabilitation association in the Southwest was given two to three psychological as well as vocational batteries to see if the student qualified for services. The student failed all of the psychological as well as vocational tests. The counselor assigned to her case did not want to recommend Susie (a fictitious name) for supported employment services. The director of the adult program suggested that the counselor observe Susie while she was actually involved in on-the-job training. The counselor observed Susie for three hours during her scheduled vocational training, and was amazed to see that Susie was able to perform better and for longer periods of time once she was performing in her actual work setting and not just on vocational psychological tests. Marc Gold (1972) notes in his vocational training literature that observing the student/client was what actually was important in measuring the student's real work abilities. He further noted that vocational assessments for persons of moderate to severe disabilities would not always be helpful since these students were often not able to perform well on such tests. Brown (1984) concurs with this view.

At the U.T. El Paso adult autism program one of the adult students with autism who was enrolled in the program was tested on a vocational test that revealed that she could not do various tasks and would therefore not be a productive work member on some job. The writer of this manuscript was given "Mary's" vocational assessment and was told by the counselor who assessed Mary that she would not be suited for vocational employment because she had tested very low on the vocational test given Mary. The writer did not place a great amount of faith in the counselors's test results and went ahead and placed Mary in vocational training in a fast food restaurant. Mary is now working ten hours a week and her hours will be increased from ten to fifteen hours in a few months. It is critical to rely on observation of a student's work potential so that an open mind concerning the student's work potential will be considered to determine the students' true work abilities.

Another aspect that is offered enough supported employment is transportation training. In this service clients are taught how to use public transportation or other means of getting to and from the job. A total of ten hours is the maximum amount of reimbursement which can be made in this category. This particular aspect of supported employment is also highly important for the student because research shows that students with disabilities often lose their jobs because they do not have adequate means of getting to and from work (Rusch, 1984). This writer has noted acting as director of the adult autism program that many Latino parents who have sons or daughters with autism and other severe handicaps do not understand the value of their youth working and therefore do not understand why they should bring them to work. The managers talk to the job coaches about the problem and job coaches speak to the parents about getting their son or daughter to work. Some of the Latino parents that this writer and job coaches have been in contact with still do not understand why they should bring their son and or daughter to work. It is through many talks with the over-protective parents and much follow-up on this particular aspect of transportation or assisting their son or daughter to go to work that eventually some parents begin to understand that it is necessary to help their son or daughter stay at work. In other cases this writer and her staff have noted that many of the parents never understand the importance of providing transportation for their son or daughter to go to work.

Another service provided by Supported Employment includes job development. In this particular category the rehabilitation commission will allow or will pay up to twenty hours for staff members to attempt to go to the community and find clients/students possible jobs. This would involve the staff speaking directly to employers and checking with employers about what jobs are available for a particular student or client. The person who is attempting to find work for the future employee will give characteristics, strengths and some weaknesses of the client so that the employer will know what job the student may be doing that he/she can match a student with. This type of job search or job development has proven very successful to the writer of this material and her staff as this process gives all concerned a feel for what is available in the community. Also, such job development or job searching allows clients who have received on-the-job training to be placed in jobs that they are capable of working at in the very near future or as soon as they need the work.

Placement is another service which is offered to clients through supported employment. This service finalizes the process of obtaining a job for a student. It may involve the service provider accompanying the client for the job interview(s). Also, the supported employment will pay for the job coach or the person who is responsible for getting the student the job for working out such details as job/task analysis, schedule of work, and getting a job description for the work the student is to do. Further, the placement category involves that the job coach or trainers discover about needed uniforms, tools, or equipment, and to work out job accommodations for the student with disabilities. Additionally the job coach will be compensated by the rehabilitation commission for preparing tax credit job forms needed to be completed for the student with disabilities. All of this needs to be done before the client/student goes to work. A maximum reimbursable amount of five hours will be paid by the rehabilitation commission for the client through supported employment monies.

Finally another important area that is reimbursable for students with severe disabilities through supported employment monies is Job Skills Training and Follow-up. This service involves orientation and training of the client at the job site. If the workcrew or enclosure trainer (in a business or industry where not more than six people with disabilities may be working) is training more than one client, the vocational counselor will negotiate an hourly rate not to exceed $20 per hour to a maximum of 200 hours.

It should be noted that in all of the categories just noted additional hours can be authorized with the different managers of the various rehabilitation commissions, depending upon individual circumstances.

Also, the services detailed in this section include nearly all the services that can be made available to vocational rehabilitation clients. Other services provided by the supported employment funds include:

Training
Maintenance
Physical and mental retardation services
Occupational licenses, tools, equipment and training supplies
Interpreter services for the deaf
Personal care attendant
Modification of vehicles, job sites and residencies

SUBMITTING VOUCHER INFORMATION
FOR RECEIVING SUPPORTED EMPLOYMENT FUNDS

After the trainer or job coach completes the total number of hours for the client through supported employment funds, the total number of hours are indicated in addition to the total amount of money which the trainer or job coach is charging on behalf of the client.

Examples of how the number of hours and totals for various categories are included below:

Example #1
Consumer and Family Orientation	(5 hours)
Job Development	(20 hours)
Transportation Training	(10 hours)
Placement	(5 hours)

Job Skills Training   (150 hours)

Total Hours: 190

Hourly Rate: $20 per hour

Total Amount of the Purchase Order:
$3,800 (190 hours × $20 per hour)

Example #2

For a client who needs only Job Development, Placement and Job Skills Training at a negotiated rate of $15 per hour, the following should be placed in the Purchase Order or form:

Job Development   (15 hours)

Placement   (5 hours)

Job Skills Training   (125 hours)

Total Hours: 145

Hourly Rate: $15 per hour

Total Amount of the Purchase Order
$2,175 (145 hours × $15 per hour)

THE INDIVIDUALIZED WRITTEN
REHABILITATION PROGRAM

A part of the Individualized Written Rehabilitation Program is the individualized transition plan which is an important plan that helps outline the services to be provided to each client served. Policies for course of the Individualized Program have generally a section for the client's name, long range vocational objective, and intermediate rehabilitation objectives (See Figure 6). There is usually a section which has the teacher or job coach trainer outline how the client's objectives will be evaluated (at least annually) using some of these criteria: job coach reports, employer's feedback, and parents' comments. Additionally there is a section in the individualized transition plan that indicates or notes the planned frequency of client contact by the trainer—every two months, for example.

Another important section in the individualized transition plan is one that denotes the actual services (See Figure 6) the clients are going to receive and the starting and ending dates for the services. Also, the client or any of the program representatives should have a section on the rehabilitation program report where comments should be provided pertaining to the success or the failure of the program. There is, further a section where the job coach trainer and/or teacher can denote which

FIGURE 6
INDIVIDUALIZED WRITTEN REHABILITATION PLAN

An example of an Individualized Written Rehabilitation Plan is presented below:

Client Name: José Chávez
Long Range Vocational Objective: Supported Employment—Service Occupations

Intermediate Rehabilitation Objectives: The client should
1. demonstrate ability to use public transportation to and from work
2. demonstrate progress on critical job tasks, and
3. demonstrate that he can stay on task for more than four hours.

Client's Progress Toward the Objectives Will Be Evaluated at Least Annually Using These Criteria:
Job Coach Reports
Employer Feedback
Parent's Comments

Planned Frequency of Client Contact:
Once every 60 days

The following specific services will be provided by the Rehabilitation Agency to assist the client in achieving the objectives. These services include any post-employment services which are expected to be needed.

FROM	TO	SERVICES
4/01/90	7/31/90	Counseling and Guidance
4/01/90	7/31/90	Supported Employment Services (210 Hours) from Sacramento MH–MR
		Consumer & Family Orientation (5 hours)
		Evaluation of Rehabilitation Potential (20 hours)
		Job Development (20 hours)
		Placement (5 hours)
		Transportation Training (10 hours)
		Job Skills Training (150 hours)
8/01/90	Duration of the Employment	Long-Term, On-Going Support provided by the Sacramento MH–MR per the signed agreement

Views of the client (and any representative) regarding this program:

It's excellent.

Client has identified and will use all comparable services and benefits which may be available:

FIGURE 6 (Continued)

_____ Medicaid   _____ Medical Insurance

_____ Medicare   _____ VA Benefits

_____ Chronically ill and Disabled Children's Services   _____ Worker's Compensation

_____ Pell Grant and/or SEOG

_____ Scholarships (specify)

_____ Other (specify)

Client participation in the cost of the planned services (if applicable):

_____

benefits should be made available, for example, Medicaid, Medicare, Medical Insurance, Scholarships, Worker's Compensation etc.. Finally, the individualized rehabilitation report will have a section where it can be noted if the client is participating in paying for some of his/her services in job training.

BEGINNING A SUPPORTED EMPLOYMENT PROGRAM

When beginning a supported employment program it is necessary to see which students or clients will be taking part. The students must be severely disabled and IQ's in the severe to profound range of mental retardation in order to qualify for supported employment funds. Also, the coordinators of the program need to talk to the Rehabilitation Commission representatives in their area so they can get financial assistance for the clients they are trying to put to work. Funds for supported employment are limited; thus, it is vital to discover the funds which are available for this type of assistance.

Also, it is important to determine who the job coaches are so that the students can be placed with trainers who will help them. Job coaches need to be chosen carefully, because many will be needed to train the clients for long periods of time. Acting as director of vocational training and adult programs, I have noted the essential qualities of a job coach:

1) The job coach should know a variety of vocational job training techniques (these have been discussed in the chapter on vocational training).
2) The job coach will need to follow the students/clients for long periods of time.
3) The job coach will need to know how to evaluate and code the clients' progress on the job.
4) The job coach will need to know names of agencies and people who are involved in possibly hiring clients with disabilities.
5) The job coach will have good communication skills, knowing how to talk to different people and agencies in the community.

As director of a vocational training project in my community, I have found that the best job coaches in the program had many of the above characteristics. Also, I has observed after having several job coaches in her adult program that many of them who train persons with severe disabilities in various jobs need to make commitments for long terms, because the process of training these students to be on their own can be quite lengthy.

ORGANIZING A SUPPORTED EMPLOYMENT PROGRAM

When beginning a supported employment program it is necessary to first find students who fit the criteria and are severely disabled. Also, it is a good idea to begin with only one or two severely handicapped clients. If one begins training with more clients than this, it will be difficult to find job coaches to train the clients. It is important to screen the clients carefully who will be selected to begin the program in supported employment. Beginning with clients one knows, who can work for long periods of time, will assure that at least some of the clients will stay on the job. Those students or clients who have been in on-the-job training programs usually make good candidates for long term success.

It is also important to discover the types of jobs that are available and are suitable for the student/clients one has selected to participate in vocational training. Talking to the community members and managers of various jobs is necessary in order to find out what jobs are available. It may be necessary to find two or three jobs in the community for each student so that each student can complete twenty hours a week. Such an arrangement is not always the best, but may be necessary in practical terms.

In the U. T. El Paso Adult Program the supported employment program was started with two students with autism. Each student had two different fast food restaurant jobs (of similar tasks) in order to have each one work for twenty hours weekly. A total of four job coaches were assigned to each of the students or clients. (The job coaches rotated so that each job coach trained the students during the time they were at work). For example, "Mary," who is 24 years old and has autism, worked ten hours at a fast food restaurant stacking dishes and trays, and worked ten hours at another fast food restaurant washing dishes and loading the automatic dishwasher. Parents were notified at the beginning of the importance of Mary getting to her two jobs on time. Because the parents were told how important it would be to get Mary to work so that she could be working a full twenty hours a week, the parents always did their best to get Mary to her jobs on time. Mary has now been working at both jobs for more than a year. It took only six months to train Mary to stay on the jobs. Part of the reason it took such a short time is because Mary had been training in several food service jobs at the University Adult Program and she had already increased her time-on-task gradually through the six month training time. In a sense, she was pre-trained for her work experience.

As the client/students are in the field working it is necessary to check the progress of the job coaches. It sometimes can happen that a job coach may begin experiencing some difficulties with the client out in the field. The job coach may not understand the importance of reporting a problem to the people who are in charge of the project, and the problem may get worse. For instance, the student or client may begin having tantrums, or may begin working less on the job. If the job coach does not inform the staff people who are directing the program, then the problem may worsen and the client could lose the job and suffer rejection as a consequence as well.

In the U. T. El Paso Adult Autism Program, "Mary," an adult student with autism, was working at Pizza Hut for ten hours weekly. At the beginning, Mary's job coach was not too aware of Mary's off-task and tantruming behavior. The job coach ignored some of Mary's initial off-task behaviors. The job coach never informed any of the staff that a problem was developing at the job site with Mary. Soon Mary's behavior became worse and the manager called the staff people and indicated that she would be losing her job if her disruptive behavior did not cease. The job coach did not cooperate with and failed to notify the staff that Mary was behaving in such a manner and Mary nearly lost her job. Following this incident the staff and job coach trainers realized that job coaches needed to be told that when they experienced trouble on the job, staff members should be informed immediately if the behavior problem did not work itself out. Often their job coaches do not know the client very well and many of the clients like Mary believe their problem will get better.

Another important component of the supported employment program is the parents. They need to be informed of the details of their son's or daughter's work schedule; the parents also need to be told whether or not the number of hours will affect the student's additional income, such as supplemental security income. (In most cases the supplemental income is not affected because the students may not work more than twenty hours a week).

This writer has learned in working with Latino parents who have sons or daughters with disabilities that often much explanation is required, simply because many do not want their son or daughter to work. They seem to believe "we will live forever!" It has been my experience that parents (and most especially Latino parents) need patient guidance, support, and instruction on many facets of work pertaining to their son or daughter. Also, I have noted that job coaches and staff have to maintain communication with parents on a long term basis while the staff is training and keeping the client on a job. Neglecting the parents can produce a problem that grows, and soon they begin to stop taking the son or daughter to work or otherwise become non-supportive, a situation which could have been prevented had someone taken the time to talk to the parents on a monthly or bi-weekly basis.

As director of the adult program I have spent as long as four years with the parents, offering them support and assistance whenever they have needed it. It takes a lot of time, planning, scheduling, and hard work to maintain communication with each parent. Usually if the parent has been well nurtured, and if staff have taken time to assist the parent, the parent will become very supportive of the son's or daughter's working and will further support the staff, even to the point of helping other parents who are about to allow their son or daughter to work.

Another important variable to consider in the area of supported employment is helping the parents understand the importance of working out transportation for their son or daughter as the job training is begun. Again, parents need to understand that their son or daughter *must* go to work. They need to be told of the possible consequences if they do not carry out their responsibilities in their son's or daughter's training. Nisbet and Hagner (1988), agree that many clients often lose the jobs that have been obtained through supported employment because transportation is not carefully worked out and parents fail to see the importance of their son or daughter being at work.

The supported employment regulations allow money to be allocated for training a client to learn to use transportation. This will be especially helpful if the client has not learned to ride the bus. It has been my experience when a person with disabilities has difficulty learning to use the bus, a family member may need to accompany the student for some of the time until the student learns to go on the bus independently. Another choice parents have is to take their son and or daughter to work daily. If specialized public transportation exists for instance El Paso, Texas, has "The Lift" (smaller buses with drivers who are trained to assist people with disabilities), then the transportation training may be much easier.

Each student who is being trained to do work should have a file developed by the staff so that all of the student's tasks, work information and personal history will be carefully documented in order to see the progress of the client during the course of training. This type of information will help agencies who are assisting with the client's training to see the actual short and long term progress of the client they are sponsoring. Evaluating the clients, trainers, and overall programming is another very important component of a supportive employment program. Every two to three months the director of the program and other staff members should sit down and decide what is working and not working in their programming with clients. This is a very healthy process and often brings to light small problems that would easily develop into major problems if left unattended. Thus bi-monthly or tri-monthly meetings of all staff members are highly encouraged so that it can be determined if the program's goals are being met.

DIFFERENT TYPES OF
SUPPORTED EMPLOYMENT OPTIONS

Some of the different supported employment options are mobile work crews, enclave, and individual options for persons with disabilities. Each of these options will be explained and some of the characteristics of each will also be noted.

Mobile Work Crews. In this particular type of employment model there are usually from three to six workers. It is a single-purpose business.

Most of the work such a crew will do is groundkeeping or janitorial work, performed in community settings. According to Wehman (1985) students with severe disabilities and behavior problems are good candidates for this type of employment.

In the mobile work crew, clients receive wages for their work, and are closely supervised by agency staff. In addition there are opportunities for community integration (e.g. clients work in "regular" office buildings, eat lunch and take their breaks in the community).

Many rural areas make good use of the mobile work crew. In Alaska and Kansas rehabilitation services have begun to develop mobile crews and plan to create more of them in the future.

The Enclave. An enclave is a group of individuals with severe disabilities who are trained and supervised to perform specific tasks but work in typical industrial settings ordinarily employing non-handicapped workers. This model maintains many of the benefits of integrated employment while providing the continuous, ongoing support that is required by some disabled individuals, particularly those with significant behavioral problems or severe disabilities, in order to achieve long term success in the job market.

Fewer states participate in the enclave model because it is expensive to maintain work enclaves. The enclave model requires a major commitment of resources in order to plan an enclave and locate a business interested in hosting it. In addition, the state agency (or provider) must be able to assume the staffing costs for the enclave supervisor, at least until the enclave has proven profitable enough for the company to become willing to assume these costs. Even so, in some states, such as California, Texas, Wisconsin and Virginia, the enclave model is used (Wehman, 1985).

The Individual Option Model. In this model the person with severe disabilities is placed to do work in different types of jobs in the community. Like in the mobile work crew and enclave, the clients will have opportunities in the different work options in the community to be around other people in order to learn appropriate social skills. In the individual work option the student may be working in a fast food restaurant, clerical, motel service, janitorial or other options which the staff may find for the student.

Acting as director of the adult program, I have had the most experience with the Individual Work Option. The director and her staff have managed to place several students with autism in fast food restaurants.

This has worked out well, because managers of fast food restaurants have been open to hiring many of the students with autism.

This writer presently has three young women with moderate to severe autism working in various fast food restaurant jobs. All have been working at their jobs for more than six months, some up to a year. Parents and staff are delighted that the supported employment model has been able to work well for the students with autism who would not have been hired had it not been for supported employment monies and good college student job coaches. According to Brown (1990) what is important is putting people to work in a meaningful work environment so that they can become productive members of society.

In conclusion, supported employment has opened the doors to many people with severe disabilities, allowing them an opportunity to work. It has also made possible for many clients with severe disabilities to have the opportunity to stay on their jobs for long periods of time.

REFERENCES

Brown, L. (1990). Vocational Programming for Persons with Severe Disabilities: presentation made at annual conference of the Association for Persons with Severe Handicaps, San Francisco.

Brown, L. (1979). A strategy for developing chronological-age appropriate and functional curricular content for severely handicapped adolescents and young adults, *Journal of Special Education* V 13, No. 1, pp. 81–90.

Brown, L. (1984). Integrated work opportunities for adults with severe handicaps: the extended training option, *JASH*, V 9, No. 4, pp. 262–269.

Federal Register (1987). Texas Rehabilitation Commission. No. 89-15 pp. 1–5.

Fredricks, B., et al. (1987). *Vocational Training for Students with Severe Handicaps.* Monmouth, OR: Teaching Research Publications, pp. 1–121.

Gold, M. (1972). "Stimulus factors in skill training of retarded adolescent on a complex assembly task: Acquisition, transfer and retention," *American Journal of Mental Deficiency* Vol. 76 pp. 517–526.

Nisbet, J. and D. Hagner (1988). "Reexamination of supported employment," *JASH*, (Vol. 13), No. 4, pp. 260–267.

Wehman, P., et al. (1977). "Behavioral training strategies in sheltered workshops for the severely developmentally disabled," *AAESPH Review* (V 2) No. 1, pp. 24–36.)

Wehman, P. (1985). "A supported employment approach to transition," *American Rehabilitation*, V 11 No. 3, pp. 12–16.

Wehman, P. (1982). "Preparing severely handicapped youth for least restrictive environments," *JASH*, V 7, No. 1, pp. 33–39.

Chapter Three

TRANSITION

This chapter will explain what transition is and will also explain the components of transition. Further, an explanation will be given of the effect of the individualized transition plan on the role of parents in the transition process.

Transition can be defined as the changes that will take place for students once they leave one program, leaving high school to begin the world of work or living outside of the home, for example. It is a term that has been used frequently in professional circles (Brown et al., 1981; Rusch & Chadsey-Rusch, 1985). The U.S. Department of Education, Office of Special Education and Rehabilitative Services (OSERS) has made transition a priority. Wehman (1986) has described vocational transition in the following manner:

> Vocational transition is a carefully planned process, which may be initiated by school personnel or by adult service providers, to establish and implement a plan for either employment or additional vocational training of a handicapped student who will graduate or leave school in three to five years; such a process must involve special educators, vocational educators, parents and/or the student, an adult service system representative, and possibly an employer.

Key aspects of this definition are that (1) members of multiple disciplines and service delivery systems must participate, (2) parental involvement is essential, (3) vocational transition planning must occur well before 21 years of age (4) the process must be planned and systematic, (5) and the vocational service must be of high quality (Halpren, 1985).

As part of transition, the term *community adjustment* is included in the definition. Community adjustment is seen as requiring competence in social and interpersonal skills and may be the most important element of all in transition. Thus, employment and independent living are important aspects of the change from school to adulthood for all students. Transition is a bridge between school and work.

Another important aspect of the definition that should be part of the definition (and one this writer has found to be often overlooked) is the cultural and linguistic components of the process, especially when planning transition for students of other languages and cultures (Durán, 1990).

According to Wehman (1988), transition is such an important process that it has been included in the Education for Handicapped Children Amendments PL98-199, under the Secondary and Transition Services Section. Section 626 of the act authorizes funds to be designated for research, training, and demonstration in the area of transition. Transition has also been a major concern of the Department of Special Education and Rehabilitative Services and has also been a focus of many articles that have appeared recently on the subject.

It has been this writer's experience that providing for transition has been slow to get started in many school districts. Many district directors of special education have indicated to this writer that they often do not have the resources to make sure that everyone's vocational goals are reached. In one district in the Southwest where this writer worked as a consultant, she realized that the various districts worked extremely slowly when they attempted to develop vocational goals which were for students to work in integrated settings. Because state mandates are now requiring transition plans, it is becoming more prevalent to see districts requiring their students to have individual plans which address the areas of transition. But districts still have much to do in the area of transition because many students presently do not have transition goals which will help them to become independent once they leave their school placements. This writer has seen too many young adults with disabilities graduate without a job or the skills needed to live independently in the community.

Some study figures on the need for transition are quite revealing: In 1983, the U.S. Commission on Civil Rights reported that between 50% and 75% of all disabled individuals were unemployed. An excellent follow-up study of disabled students in Vermont (Hasazi, Gordon & Roe, 1985) reflects similar figures of unemployment, as do the preliminary results of a follow-up study underway in Virginia (Wehman, Kregel, & Sayfarth, 1985). In Colorado another follow-up study indicates that although over 60% of the recent special education graduates are working, there was a high level of underemployment and very poor wages (Mithaug, Horiuchi, and Fanning, 1985). Attempted solutions to this problem have received federal incentives through P.L. 98-199, the Education for Handicapped Children Amendments. These amendments provide funds and support for secondary education and transitional services.

Similarly, another study was conducted of secondary special education programs in Oregon (Halpren, 1985), and it was discovered by the parents noted that less than 50% of their children received instruction in such important areas as vocational preparation, functional academics, home living skills, and community living skills. Also, the same survey revealed that teachers felt the students with severe disabilities could not be mainstreamed, according to them, because the students lacked entry skills. The regular class teachers resisted the students being mainstreamed, and supported resources were not available for the students.

According to (Lipsky 1985), parental influence is a major contributor to the lack of employment. Parents of youth with disabilities are, of course, no less subject than the general public to the negative messages our society presents of persons with disabilities. Yet, just as parents of youth with disabilities are "labeled," focusing on them as an impediment to employment of youth with disabilities may be easier than holding the system responsible. The poor track record of schools and other service agencies in treating parents honestly and with respect gives legitimate cause for parental caution, if not suspicion. Parents' fears about loss of benefits for the most part are not idle, nor are their concerns about risks for their children unfounded. Also, the reports that youth with disabilities continue to live at home well into their twenties (and beyond) make effective parental involvement all the more consequential.

According to (Lipsky 1988), the following recommendations have been made to encourage youth and parental involvement:

1) Enhancing youth's self concept and self confidence, by improving education and training programs, to prepare youth with disabilities for post-school employment, community living, and full citizenship.
2) Recognizing youth's autonomy entitlement and decision-making capacity, reflected in involvement in IEP or individualized education plan development, decisions as to training and employment opportunities, and other aspects of their lives.
3) Training of youth in and encouragement of self-advocacy activities.
4) Developing mutual support activities for both youth and parents.
5) Developing mentoring programs involving adults with disabilities.
6) Developing public awareness programs as to the achievements of persons with disabilities.

7) Involving parents in ways that reflect their legitimate concerns, substantial knowledge; and adult.

8) Adult training of parents reciprocally with service providers.

Obviously, the importance of the involvement of parents goes beyond transition activities; it is essential to the entire education program of children.

According to (Lipsky 1985), parents were the major force in the passage of P.L. 94-142. While sometimes viewed by professionals in negative ways, parents have been increasingly recognized as playing a substantial role in the effective education of children. Thus, parents who have a blind child become parents who are "blind parents," or the parents who have a child who has spina bifida become "spina bifida parents."

Lipsky (1985) further noted that parents are not involved in their son's or daughter's education.

Summarizing a number of studies of parents, one review states that these reports suggest that up to half of the parents fail to participate ...(Meyers & Blacher, 1987). One study reported that in 70% of the cases, parents provided no input to IEP development (A National Survey, 1980). Another study reports that only half of the parents attended IEP meetings (Scanlon, Arick, and Phelps, 1981), and that when they did, professionals believed that they contributed little (Goldstein, Strickland, Turnbull, & Carry, 1980; Lynch & Stein, 1982).

In contrast, the Louis Harris study reports that 79% of the parents said they attended their child's most recent IEP conference, while 9% reported that they were not informed of the meeting or that the school did not offer such meetings. Among those parents who participated in the IEP conferences, 73% felt they contributed to the development of objectives for their children's IEP, 60% felt that the IEP goals "very much" reflected their child's needs, and only 20% felt that the goals of their child's IEP were not being properly carried out.

There are some data to suggest that parents of more severely impaired children participate more in the IEP process (Meyers & Blacher, 1987; Morgan, 1980), while those with less severely impaired children are less involved in the process (McKinney & Hocutt, 1982).

Another set of factors affecting the extent of parental involvement concerns race, class, and education. A study of four city school districts found, "a white, married mother who graduated from high school was 5.4 times more likely than a nonwhite, single mother who had not graduated from high school, to have attended the most recent IEP conference held for her child" (Singer & Butler, 1987).

Several studies indicate that parents "feel intimidated or are provided only limited opportunity" to become involved (Meyers & Blacher, 1987). This situation is true even when the parents are themselves professionals (Turnbull & Turnbull, 1978). And this point is emphasized in a Department of Education report to Congress which notes that parents had no pre-conference input, and "several studies have reported that in the majority of IEP conferences, the IEP was completely prepared prior to the meeting . . . " The report concludes by saying that "presenting parents with what may appear to be decisions the school has already reached rather than recommendations, and the failure to directly communicate and provide opportunities for involvement, can obviously limit parent participation in the IEP decision making process," (Ninth Annual Report, 1987).

Several factors appear to account for this limited involvement of parents in the IEP process. They include such factors as (1) parents' desire not to participate, (2) parents' inability to participate, or (3) parents' belief that the school does not welcome them. These factors are as true for parents of children without disabilities as for those with them. For example, a recent national study reports from one-fifth to one-third of all parents either never or only once a year participate in any activity involving their child's school (Strengthening Links, 1987).

The Louis Harris survey reports the highest level of parental dissatisfaction concerns the transition from school to work; only 44% of the parents said it was "effective." This judgment is not surprising given the report of parents of children 17 years of age or older that a transition plan was a part of the IEP in only 38% of the cases, that job counseling and placement occurred in 40% of the cases, and contact with a vocational rehabilitation agency occurred in only 43% of the cases (The ICD Survey III, 1990).

Parents are often absent from the transition as well as from the educational process of the child. Some of the reasons that parents are often absent from the educational process of their son or daughter include the nature of professional response to parents (Gartner, 1988; Lipsky, 1985), the lack of support for families (Lipsky, 1985), and the inappropriateness of the service arrangements. For instance, only 6 percent of Oregon districts had formal written agreements with other agencies to coordinate transition services, and 15 percent of the districts had no coordination mechanisms (Benz & Halpren, 1987). Equally rare are efforts to see parents as possessors of valuable knowledge about their child's employment potential or as potential "trainers" of the professionals (Gartner, 1988), or to ascertain from parents what information parents need to be effective participants in the transition process. (Liebert et al., 1987).

Latino parents, for example, in the Southwest (where this writer worked closely with several families) seldom attended the IEP meetings of their son or daughter. Many of them felt they did not understand English well enough to comprehend what was happening during the meetings. Also many of the Latino parents noted that they did not feel their views were valued at the IEP meeting. Several expressed their fears that they were not smart enough to be able to contribute their views about their son or daughter.

There are some further recommendations that can be made for families who have sons or daughters with disabilities. Some of the recommendations include

1) Reaching out to the family early so they can become involved with their son's or daughter's education. This early initiation will be helpful to professionals who are trying to get services for these students.

2) If families need an array of services by different agencies this information should be made available to the families. This universal access is important to the families so they can access services from the different agencies.

3) Services for families should be individualized, because every family will need different as well as similar services for their family members who have disabilities.

4) Supports offered to the families should emphasize their strengths rather than focus on deficits.

5) Families should be given opportunities to share their similar experiences. By sharing these experiences they can often build bonds that are needed in order for them to receive the mutual support that only other families who are experiencing similar experiences can share with one another.

6) Families need to be praised for their knowledge of their sons' and daughters' needs; thus some of the family wishes should be given consideration and priority.

7) Professionals and parents need to define and give meaning to the

partnership they are to do together when working with their son or daughter. Both parents and professionals have important information which needs to be shared among all who are concerned with the child's development. Partnership includes mutual respect, sharing in a common purpose, joint decision-making, sharing feelings, and flexibility in dealing with each other (Lipsky, 1989).

COMPONENTS OF TRANSITION

Transition involves vocational, leisure, and living options for the student with moderate to severe disabilities. The first area that will be discussed is the vocational options.

The chapters on supported employment and vocational training have given many of the different work options which make up the transition process; here, the work options will be presented briefly as a review of the vocational opportunities which make up transition.

Some of the work options students can do in transition are mobile work crews, enclaves, competitive employment, and other work options in the community.

Each of these particular work options is part of the student's individualized transition plan. The individualized transition plan outlines what type of work the student will be performing. More will be explained concerning the individualized transition plan.

Often, vocational training for developmentally disabled youth does not begin until they are 15–16 years of age. Because many youth with disabilities learn tasks very slowly, vocational experiences should begin early and should continue through the school years. Early vocational emphasis can mean that the student will receive some on-the-job training which is functional, integrated and can also include on-the-job training.

In the vocational program this writer coordinated, many of the students with autism and other severe handicaps received on-the-job training in such locations as the university food service, convalescent or nursing center, alumni office at a university, and other types of jobs that could be found by checking around the campus, and nearby areas of the school and university were utilized by the students. The students started much of their vocational training twice weekly for an hour each day when they were approximately twelve or thirteen years old, as part of their individualized transition plan. During the preliminary individualized education plan meeting, the parents often requested that their son or daughter begin training on-the-job when they reached the age of 12 or 13. It was discovered by the director of the program and the teachers that students who started training at age 12 were more proficient in staying on the job once they left their public school programming than those students who started on-the-job training later, when they were 17 or 18 years old, for example. This advantage was especially true for students with autism who started their training at age 11 or 12. Many of the students who did train early are presently on their jobs several years later, and are doing very nicely working a few hours during the week. Employers have commented that the students, especially students with autism, benefit the most from early intervention in vocational training as well as additional other areas of the curriculum.

The other areas of transition, such as leisure and living arrangements, are also important. Too often students graduate from high school and do not know how to engage in play or leisure activities that will help them add activities to their lives.

In the adult transition program that this writer coordinated at U.T. El Paso, every day the students were given choices of activities they could engage in.

Some were allowed to choose from playing ball activities, jumping rope, playing activities such as relay races, and other activities that were part of the students' families. For example, some of the students enjoyed playing baseball and volleyball. This writer made certain that activities the students chose from were part of the various activities that the students participated in at home or in their neighborhoods. When it was not certain what they participated in at home, the director and teacher helped the families fill out a questionnaire on leisure activities (see Figure 7) to determine what activities, if any, the students engaged in with their families. Since many of the families we had in the university program were from poor Latino families, when the questionnaires were completed it was discovered that many of the families and students did not participate in activities that would help them develop their choice making capacities, nor did they participate in game or funlike activities. When the students started to learn activities in the program, the parents became happy because they noticed their sons and daughters started doing new activities at home.

It is important to discover what families are doing or not doing at home with the various areas of the curriculum. If only those activities

FIGURE 7

LEISURE ACTIVITY INVENTORY INVENTARIO DE OCIO

1. Which activities does your son and/or daughter do after school?

1. ¿En que actividades participa su hijo o hija después de la escuela?

2. Does your son or daughter play alone or with neighbor children?

2. ¿Participa su hijo o hija con otros niños o amigos de la vecindad o juega solo?

3. If you could teach your son and/or daughter activities, what would you teach him/her to play?

3. ¿Si pudiera enseñarle a su hijo o hija actividades, que le enseñaría?

are taught at schools or in other programs which the teacher would like to encourage students to learn, the students will not transfer many of the activities to their homes, because they do not do these leisure activities at home.

Leisure activities need to be planned for in the student's individualized education or transition plan; otherwise, this is an area that can be easily overlooked for the student. Parents need to be enlightened on the importance of including such a component in the plan of the student. Many Latino parents, for example, believed leisure activities are not in the student's best interest because, culturally speaking, many Latino parents value their son or daughter learning academic subjects, and believe that if their children play or such engage in activities they will not learn to be productive citizens.

By explaining to Latino parents that their son or daughter would not lose anything by participating in leisure activities, some of the parents became more supportive at their students' individualized plan meeting. Time must be taken with parents if they are to give the support that is needed for their sons and daughters education.

Another component of transition is providing living options for persons with disabilities. Some of the living possibilities for persons with disabilities include staying or remaining at home, living in group homes in the community, living in supervised apartments, and/or living in supervised twenty-four hour facilities.

It has been this writer's experience that this is the most difficult component of transition. Parents do not often have adequate information on what their options are for placing their son or daughter in a home or apartment once their family member graduates from school. The family often would like their son or daughter to live in another home other than the one their family member grew up in, if they knew what options exist.

In some instances the family member may remain at home; in other cases it is best for the son or daughter to live away from the parents. By living away from the parents, often times the son or daughter learns more independence. Also, in some instances the family member, as in some cases students with severe autism, may need to be placed in an all day care facility in order to get the best help possible for their son or daughter.

As director of the adult transition program this writer witnessed many parents who had sons and daughters with severe autism; these parents often were not able to live with their son/daughter with severe autism and as a result they were extremely nervous and tense about where they would place their son or daughter with autism. Several felt that they were going to go insane if they could not get some relief by having their son or daughter out of the house temporarily. Once the parents were given information on costs and the types of residential facilities which were available for their family member, they were better able to make choices for their son or daughter.

One of the most important components of the transition process is the individualized transition plan. The individualized transition plan outlines for a student what his/her program will be in the areas of vocational, leisure and residential options. It further notes who will be responsible for training the student and what the dates are when the proposed training will be started and completed. The starting age of the student in the transition planning is also noted. Presently many states, for example Texas, California, and Oregon, have a suggested age of 16 years for the student to begin transition. According to (Everson & Moon 1987) the suggested age for beginning transition may be 16, but the actual transition process should begin before that time. In many instances, parents are wisely requesting transition services to begin before the 16 year age limit.

The individualized transition plan also indicates which community agencies will be responsible for the student's training in the community. When a transition plan is not used by a district to outline services for a student, then many districts, like in California, utilize the individualized education plan to outline transition services. Wehman (1988) notes that it is his recommendation that transition goals and planning be a separate part of the individualized education program. Wehman feels that, in order for transition planning to be successful, it needs to be a separate part of the individualized education plan.

A transition plan sample is indicated in Figure 8. A good transition plan will include the components listed in Figure 8. It is important to note who will be the person(s) responsible for carrying out the training. If this detail is not stipulated, there may be confusion later.

It has further been the experience of this writer that it is extremely valuable to note who will be responsible for the various components of transition so that not only will it be known who will do what training, but will also be an excellent opportunity to meet with the people or agency people responsible for carrying out the various components of transition. Without good communication among agency people, it will not be possible to plan appropriate transition services for the students. Agency planning and cooperation are essential to the successful transition process. Agency planning and communication also avoid unnecessary duplication of services for students.

Also, as part of the transition process, parents should be made aware of the employment alternatives available for their son or daughter upon graduation. Further, parents need to be helped to understand the individualized transition process. If parents are well informed, the individualized transition process, that is, individualized transition plan meetings, will be better attended, and parents will participate in the process more efficiently. If parents have concerns, teachers and other professionals can help answer their questions by having conferences and meetings.

According to Wehman (1988), parent education meetings should (1) give information to parents of what is available in the community, (2) explain to parents what vocational training, vocational education and transition are, and (3) prepare parents to work with various agencies to develop transition plans.

This writer has also noted in working with various Latino families in the Southwest and has observed as in working with consultants that the parents did not understand various terms that were presented to them frequently at school and on-the-job training. To meet this problem, meetings were held where each term was defined in Spanish as well as English. Additionally, parents were given several examples in Spanish of whatever concept was being presented to them so they could better understand each of the concepts. For example, the word "transition" was usually difficult for the parents to understand. First, we would say to the parent(s), "¿Sabe lo que quiere decir la palabra transición?" ("Do you

FIGURE 8
SAMPLE OF INDIVIDUALIZED TRANSITION PLAN

Name of Student: _____

Date of graduation: _____ Age: _____ Date of Birth: _____

Employment Goals: _Part-time employment at Pizza Hut_____

Person Responsible: _____

Starting Date: _____ Ending Date: _____

Agency(s) responsible: _____

Residential Goals: __Placement in group home before student graduates from high school.__

Person Responsible: _____

Starting Date: _____ Ending Date: _____

Agency Involved: _____

Recreation/Leisure Goals: __Participation in exercise class at local YWCA._____

Person Responsible: _____

Starting Date: _____ Ending Date: _____

Agency(s) Responsible: _____

Other Goals: __To learn to ride the city bus_____

Person Responsible: _____

Starting Date: _____ Ending Date: _____

Agency(s) Responsible: _____

Other team members: _____

Parent or Guardian: _____ Suggested Review Date: _____

know what transition means?") "Transición es el proceso donde su hijo o hija va a prepararse para su vida de trabajo, vivir, y recreación." ("Transition is the process by which your son or daughter will prepare for work, living, and recreation.")

In order not to overwhelm parents, it is important to explain the different components of transition carefully, making certain that parents know the different options they can make in the areas of vocational, residential, leisure, and recreation decisions.

Further, parents need to be made aware that transition should begin early in order for their son or daughter to have an opportunity to become employed, live in the community, and work. In the adult transition program parents often became overwhelmed if they were told too much information concerning choices they could make for their sons or daughters in the transition process. Gradually, as parents met with the professionals on a monthly basis, they began to understand the different components of the individualized transition plan.

WHAT SCHOOLS AND PARENTS DO TO ENHANCE TRANSITION

The importance of beginning vocational training, which is a major part of transition, cannot be overlooked. Throughout this chapter and other chapters within this book, it is stressed that vocational training as well as other areas which enhance independence in the students must begin early. Below will be a discussion of what types of programming and activities should be developed by the elementary, middle school, senior high school, and post secondary programs for students with disabilities. Such programming requires consistency, patience, careful scheduling, and frequent conferring with a variety of professionals. The more ideas can be discussed and talked about with all parties concerned, the greater will be the success of the planning (Wehman, 1985; Durán, 1990).

Elementary Level

1) Look around the classroom, school, school grounds and campus and discover what types of jobs your students could get training in. For example, in the classroom the students could learn to empty trash cans, dust furniture, arrange books on shelves, and clean chalk boards. Also, some of the classrooms often need the floors swept before the end of the day.

2) Have students identify and purchase items with money. If they do not purchase item(s) at the store at least one time weekly, teaching them money recognition will not be helpful. Skills must not be

taught in isolation; otherwise, no generalization will occur (Brown, 1990).

3) On the playground, students can pick up some paper and other trash items and separate the material so it can be recycled.

4) In the school offices, students can collate, file, stuff envelopes, staple materials, dust furniture around the offices, and water indoor plants.

5) In the cafeterias, students can stack trays, load dishwashers, clean tables, and arrange milk cartons so that students can place the carton of milk on their trays. Students can also assist with some of the general sweeping and bussing of the tables.

6) In the school libraries, students can help place books on appropriate shelves. Librarians can allow students to arrange magazines and other materials on tables and shelves.

7) Individual inventories must be taken monthly to reassess what further could be accomplished by students.

8) Teachers must alert people in and around the school so that new job training possibilities can be found.

9) As students get older teachers can extend the amount of training and amount of time in doing any of the above activities. Parents should be encouraged to have their son or daughter do similar activities at home, in order for generalization to occur.

10) The vocational activities must be planned (Wehman, 1985; Durán, 1990).

Middle School

Many of the above vocational training ideas can be easily continued once the student reaches middle school years. Again, as the student becomes older, more of the activities that the students can do can be added and the time the student spends in the activities can also be increased. For example, if the students were doing some of the vocational training activities for one hour once a week during elementary school, the time could be increased to two hours twice weekly. The amount of time that students do activities in vocational training depends on the student and other educational training that must be accomplished for the student. If the students have had practice doing activities during elementary school, it will be easier for them to do vocational training activities for longer periods of time during the middle school years.

Some of the students with autism begin to go through puberty during the middle years, and vocational training may become difficult because of tantruming behavior students may exhibit. If the vocational training is started in the elementary schools, then students will be better prepared to learn to do a variety of tasks, and less time will be spent in actual training of the students to learn to do work.

This writer has noted that by the time students reach this level, if they have not learned to stay on task and complete various vocational training tasks, it will be difficult for the student to progress because so many of the students' behaviors have been set, and it is difficult to modify students' behaviors especially if they have severe autism or other severe developmental disabilities. By the time the students have reached their middle years or are beginning adolescence, many of their work behaviors or lack of having work behaviors become very evident. This is why the importance of beginning vocational training early during the elementary years cannot be overlooked (Wehman, 1985; Durán, 1990).

Secondary School

The secondary years should be years that are extensions of training that has been initiated in the elementary and middle school years. By this time, students should be working more time on the job, and many will have part time employment. The jobs the students can do are food service, clerical, janitorial, working on fast food restaurants, motel service, and any other jobs that the teacher, parent, job coach or other participant can develop or creatively discover for the students in his/her area. During the high school years, the amount of vocational training and/or job training should be increased to half a day or even an entire day by the time the student is completing secondary school.

According to Brown (1990), as the students are older more time should be spent by the student in vocational training, and less time should be spent by the student in the classroom. Students with mental retardation, especially those with severe mental retardation and or autism, require more time to learn to stay on task. A good job trainer will understand this and will add the necessary vocational training to the student's work schedule in order for the student to master the importance of following directions and staying on task.

Postsecondary Programming

This is one of the most often neglected areas in vocational training, mainly because at that time many students remain at home, and little attention is given to them once they leave the public schools.

This writer directed an adult transition program in the Southwest for more than six years. In this adult program many students came to the doors of the university program to get services because they had often been at home without any kind of services for several years. The program had as a goal to help students learn job training skills in order to get jobs in the community. Most of the students in the program had severe autism or were students with severe to profound mental retardation. There was always a long waiting list of students who needed to be enrolled in the program.

The program consisted of teaching students various job skills through training in the university and job sites around the community. Students who had just graduated from the public schools were often able to get a job in the community within a few months. Many students who had been sitting at home for several years required additional training before they were able to begin to do their work in the community. Several who had been out of school for extended periods of time were unable to stay on a job or job training for very long, because they did not have the appropriate on-task skills. It has been noted by (Lovaas 1981) that students with severe autism and other developmental disorders must be in training twenty-four hours a day; otherwise, they begin to lose skills daily. Few programs are able to assist the students with autism and other severe disabilities, and, as a result, students often do not get the services they need and do not become part of the working population. This writer can say without hesitation that the students with the severe disabilities are often the most neglected students of any group in the population. This writer has not heard of many programs which are designed to specifically help the student with severe disabilities. The literature often includes reports of the students with mild disabilities being put to work, but little is ever heard of the student with severe disabilities who becomes part of the work force. It is essential that there be help given to this most neglected group through post secondary services.

Through the years in the program this writer directed more than fifteen students with autism and other severe disabilities who were put to work for pay in the community. Useful productive employment—even for those with autism and severe disabilities—is possible, if the people who should be involved are able to do their jobs. Post secondary vocational training is essential because too many students are sitting at home after they graduate from high school.

Follow-Up

Another major component of the transition process is follow-up. Follow-up is extremely critical if one is to see how effective the training and transition efforts through the years have been with students. Follow-up with students should continue as long as possible. Five or more years is recommended by most authorities.

Follow-up allows program coordinators, teachers, parents, administrators, and other community care and service providers to see if the skills taught in the program previously are effectively assisting students so they can work once they leave high school placements. Follow-up also helps transition program coordinators to determine if the programming they are doing with their students is helping students stay on their jobs during the long run. Transition follow-up in many ways is like a program evaluation, in that it reveals to program coordinators the good and positive things about a vocational program, and it also reveals what are the weaknesses of the program.

In one follow-up study that was done by (Chadsey-Rusch 1990), for example, it was determined that training in work skills for students with disabilities needs to include social interactions. Some of the social skills or desirable social behavior that they found was needed among students with disabilities was

1) Reciting full name.
2) Following instructions.
3) Asking for assistance.
4) Responding to criticism.
5) Getting information before a job.
6) Offering help to co-workers.

After this particular follow-up study was completed, the students started to receive more training from the teachers including activities in the community which stressed more social interaction in the work place and during leisure time activities.

Another example of where transition follow-up was helpful was in a review of programming that was done by (McDonnell and Hardman 1991). In this study it was revealed that more needed to be stressed in the vocational training programs concerning residential options for students with disabilities. Also, the questionnaire completed in the same study revealed that more planning needed to be done for leisure activities.

Thus, transition planning includes components of work, leisure, and living options, and also includes an individualized transition plan which outlines for the student these particular goals. Further the transition process includes follow-up, which assists everyone involved in the transition process to plan more effectively for the student. This, after all, is the main objective of the transition process—to assist students to become active participants in the world of work, living, and leisure.

REFERENCES

Benz, M. R. & A. S. Halpren (1987). Transition services for secondary students with mild disabilities: A statewide perspective. *Exceptional Children*, 53 (6), 507–514).

Brown, L. et al. (1981). Longitudinal transition plans in programs for severely handicapped students. *Exceptional Children*, 47(8), 624–630.

Chadsey, J. & F. R. Rush (1960). Social interactions of secondary-aged students with severe handicaps: implications for facilitating the transition from school to work. *JASH*, Vol. 15, n. 2, 69–78.

Durán, E. (1990). "Transition, Employment and Other Issues for Hispanic Families," (presentation made at CALTASH Conference), Sacramento, CA, Spring, 1990.

Everson, J. M. & S. Moon (1987). Transition services for young adults with severe disabilities: defining professional and parental roles and responsibilities. *JASH*, Vol. 12, No. 2, 87–95.

Gartner, A. (1988). Parents, no longer excluded, just ignored: Some ways to do it nicely. *Exceptional Parent*, Vol. 18 No. 1, 41–42.

Goldstein, S., B. Strickland, A. P. Turnbull & L. Carry (1980). An observational analysis of the IEP conference. *Exceptional Children*, 46, 278–286.

Halpren, A. S. (1985). Transition: A look at the foundations. *Exceptional Children*, Vol. 51, No. 6, 479–486.

Hasazi, S., L. Gordon & C. Roe (1985). Factors associated with the employment status of handicapped youth exiting high school from 1979 to 1983. *Exceptional Children*, 51, 455–469.

Liebert, D., D. K. Lipsky & M. Horowitz (1987). "Identification of parent needs for transition planning." Unpublished manuscript.

Lipsky, D. K. (1985). A parental perspective on stress and coping. *American Journal of Orthopsychiatry*. 55 (4), 614–617.

Lipsky, D. K. (1989). Equity and Excellence for all Students, presentation before the National Council on Disability National Study on the Education of Students with Disabilities. "Where Do We Stand?" City University of New York. pp. 19–52.

Lipsky, D. K. (1988). *Strategies for Overcoming Barriers to Employment for Youth with Disabilities*. Final Report, Mary E. Switzer Distinguished Fellow, National Institute on Disability and Rehabilitation Research. New York: The Graduate School and University Center, The City University of New York.

Lovaas, I. (1981). *Teaching Developmentally Disabled Children: The Me Book.* Baltimore: University Park Press.

McDonnell, J. & M. Hardman (1991). "Planning the transition of severely handicapped youth from school to adult services: A framework for high school programs, *Education and Training of the Mentally Retarded,* Vol. 3.

McKinney, J. D., & A. Hocutt (1982). Public school involvement of parents of learning disabled and average achievers. *Exceptional Children Quarterly,* Vol. 3, pp. 64–73.

Meyers, C. E. & J. Blacher (1987). Parents' perceptions of schooling of severely handicapped children: Home and family variables. *Exceptional Children,* Vol. 53 No. 5, 441–449.

Mithaug, D., C. Horiuchi & P. Fanning (1985). A report on the Colorado statewide follow-up survey of special education students. *Exceptional Children,* Vol. 51, pp. 397–404.

Ninth Annual Report to the Congress on the Implementation of the Education of the Handicapped Act (1987). Washington, DC: U. S. Department of Education.

Rusch, F. R. & J. Chadsey (1985). Employment for persons with severe handicaps: Curriculum development and coordination of services, *Focus on Exceptional Children,* Vol. 17 No. 9, 1–8.

Scanlon, C. A., J. Arick & N. Phelps (1981). Participation in the development of the IEP: Parents perspective. *Exceptional Children,* 47, 370–375.

Singer, J. D. & J. A. Butler (1987). The Education for All Handicapped Children Act: Schools as agents of social reform: *Harvard Education Review,* Vol. 57 No. 2, pp. 125–152.

Turnbull, A. P. & H. P. Turnbull (1978). *Parents Speak Out: Views from the Other Side of the Mirror.* Columbus, OH: Charles E. Merrill.

Wehman, P. et al. (1988). *Transition From School to Work — New Challenges for Youth with Severe Disabilities.* Baltimore: Paul Brookes.

Wehman, P., J. Kregel & J. Sayfarth (1985). A follow-up of mentally retarded graduates' vocational and independent living skills in Virginia. *Rehabilitation Counseling Bulletin.*

Chapter Four

COMMUNITY-BASED INSTRUCTION

This chapter will define community-based instruction and information given on elements that make up community-based instruction. The writer will share some direct information which she has used to do community-based instruction with persons with severe disabilities.

WHAT IS COMMUNITY-BASED INSTRUCTION?

Community-based instruction has been defined as teaching relevant, critical activities in the setting and/or natural environment where they most frequently occur in the student's community or daily living plan.

Community-based instruction requires much planning and coordination with the families of the students participating in the instruction. It also requires much planning with the staff and school administrators in order to achieve overall effectiveness for the program.

HOW TO ORGANIZE A COMMUNITY-BASED PROGRAM

Teachers and staff must be excited about understanding such a program. This writer has observed that teachers and instructional aides who are not excited about being in the community with their students will not do as well as staff members who are excited about being in the community. Enthusiasm and excitement causes others to be excited.

Staff must also do an ecological inventory to discover what is in the student's community. For instance what stores, restaurants, public shops and so on are located in the community? What stores, shops, and restaurants are in the student's immediate community? This is important to consider because the students need to train to use shops, restaurants, and other public facilities in their local communities, both where they live and where their schools are located. Once these facilities are located in their school environment and their home environment training must be planned so the students can frequent these areas as often as can be, as planned by the teacher.

Parents need to be involved being given full information about the places they can take their children, and how to lead them into appropriate experiences and behaviors.

Another component to consider when organizing a community-based program is that parents and teachers need to be given training so they can know what community-based instruction is. Also parents and staff need techniques so they can know how to teach their sons/daughters/ students important strategies to follow in the communities.

TRAINING PARENTS AND STAFF TO DO COMMUNITY-BASED INSTRUCTION

A possible outline to follow when conducting a workshop to teach parents and staff may be as follows:

1) Define Community-Based Instruction.
2) Explain the Importance of Community-Based Instruction.
3) Demonstrate How to Teach Students to Use the Community.
4) Explain the Parent's Role in Community-Based Instruction.
5) Share a Slide Presentation of Another Program Involved in Community-Based Instruction.
6) Provide Training Techniques
   A. Picture Booklets
   B. Prompt (Ford, Miranda 1984)
      Verbal
      Physical Guidance
      Gestures
      Combination of all of the above
      Photographs
      Standing Behind Client or Student
      Task Analysis
7) Provide for Generalization Training.
8) Explain Data Analysis/Evaluation.
9) Call for Questions/Discussion.

The value of giving such workshops cannot be underestimated. It is possible the staff may want to give a separate workshops to parents and to the professionals or staff. The person(s) coordinating such training will be the best judge of this decision. Regardless of whether the workshop is done jointly or separated, it is important to take time to plan such a workshop because this preparation will assist the teacher with many of the long range objectives of the program. If parents and staff understand what they are doing, then they will give more support to the program.

If parents speak one language fluently, such as Spanish, they should be given a workshop in their native language so they can better understand all that is being proposed in the community-based program.

Parents, especially if Latino, should be allowed to be in small groups as part of their workshop so they can participate more openly and be less shy or reserved. Small group instruction composed of 3 or 4 parents in each group will allow Latino parents especially to be more open and share their experiences more freely. Parents who are in these smaller groups also ask more questions if they do not understand what they are being presented. In small groups the staff can also check to see which parents do not understand what is being presented in the training. It is much easier to note in small groups what parents do not understand or are not clear on any of the points discussed in the workshop.

Staff members have also commented to the writer that a pre-training workshop is helpful because professionals and teachers received actual demonstration of what to do with each part of the training. Too often we assume that teachers and other professionals understand what we have shown them in a small lecture-type presentation and the results are evident when staff members are unclear as to what to do because there has been no modeling or demonstration for staff members. Modeling and demonstration are very necessary components when attempting to give staff members and parents new information and skills.

SCHEDULING

When considering scheduling of the students who are going to be in the community it is important to consider the ages of the students and where the sites are located. The age of the student is an important factor because all too often the students are in their late adolescence or early twenties, and students will soon be graduating from the public schools and thus will need to be in the community, for example they will need to experience different stores and restaurants in the community.

This writer has too often seen many students with severe disabilities not adequately prepared in the community because they were not taken to different stores to shop and buy items while in the public schools. With some Latino families, for example, it becomes critical to take these students out to the community because they would not get an opportunity to experience certain challenges in their homes. Many Latino families do not take their sons and or daughters to the store or restaurant because the parents are afraid the students will have a temper tantrum and they feel they will not know how to explain to others what is taking place with their sons or daughters.

Further, many Latino families have large families and to add another person to do the shopping trip would be too much for the families to manage a child with disabilities. Parents of the mother will often become caretakers of the sons or daughters with disabilities at home or the child will be taken care of at home by sisters.

The older student should be scheduled to frequent stores and restaurants at least two to three times weekly. The teachers or the staff members should discover what stores and restaurants are near the student's homes so that parents can be encouraged to take their sons/daughters to stores and restaurants and other public places near their homes. This training based upon home neighborhoods helps with generalization training. Generalization training is necessary for persons with severe disabilities. Another important aspect to consider as part of the scheduling is for the teacher to make everything clear to the parents so all concerned can know where the students will be going. Parents can often assist with some of the training, and they can also suggest other places their son and or daughter may need to go in the community.

Additionally, when the teacher is scheduling activities for the students to complete, it is necessary for the teacher or staff to make a chart kept in a centralized place indicating where the class will be from the beginning of the day until the end. For example, if the teacher, staff, and some volunteer parents will be guiding the students to various restaurants and stores from 10:30 a.m. to 11:45 a.m., this should be noted on a chart (See Figure 9). The chart should be kept up to date or as is needed by the class and or staff. This writer has noted the need for translation of the various entries on the chart in to both English and Spanish. Often parents may come to the classroom to find out where their sons/daughters are in the community. Obviously, administrators of the school or program specialists and or consultants may also need to know where the class has gone during a particular day.

Scheduling involves not only selecting different sites for the students

FIGURE 9
Adult Transition Program
Schedule of Activities

Programa de Transcisión
Orario de Actividades

8:30–Noon
(Ocho y media hasta las doce
del día)

Get ready for bus or cars (Listos para el camión.)

Meet bus at bus stop.
Encontrar al camión.

Get money ready and communication booklets and picture cards.
Tenga listo su dinero, libros de comunicación y fotos.

Go to Safeway.
Vaya a Safeway.

Go to Seven-Eleven Convenient Store
Vaya a la tienda Seven-Eleven.

Eat Lunch at Kentucky Fried Chicken
Vaya a comer a Kentucky Fried Chicken.

1:00 p.m.–3:30 p.m.
(De la una a las tres y media)

Visit to Drugstore
Vaya a la botica.

Vocational training in various sites in the community.
Entrenamiento de vocación en la comunidad.

to shop or eat in weekly, but it also involves noting the number of the students in the class. Also it is important to let administrators know where the class will be during a particular morning or afternoon. Finally, when scheduling is done it is necessary to rotate the community sites where the students will be going from week to week.

Another consideration which needs to be made when considering the scheduling of students is to note the staff/student ratio. For every student who has impairments which are severe in nature, for example, noncomplaint behavior or severe self mutilation as self abuse, there should be one adult per student. If the student's problem is less severe in nature, the ratio can be two students per one adult. Preferably there should always be a minimum staff ratio of one adult per two students.

It has been this writer's experience that students with severe impairment problems or behavior difficulties who are not well supervised in the community will not profit from the various activities which the teacher has planned for the students. Students with autism, for instance, often need to be physically guided so they can complete their tasks. Usually if a student with autism is taken to the community and the student is extremely non-compliant a single staff person will not be able to have the student complete the work. It will take two staff persons to achieve successful completion of the experience.

According to Brown (1991) when deciding on how much staff to have accompany these students, it is a good idea to note what the day will be like with all the students in the community before the teacher and aide take students out to the community. Also, the staff should make note how many students there will be per adult. By doing this ahead of time the teacher will be able to anticipate problem areas with certain students and will note which students will need special guidance and help with additional staff members. Having a mental vision or map associated with the client will help the teacher each time to visualize the entire picture of community instruction when, the teacher is to be out in the community with the students. Such planning will prevent some students from being improperly supervised in the community.

Once the staff and student ratio have been worked out, scheduling must also include how often the students will be shopping or eating at various areas in the community. In order to decide how this will be done, the teacher should note what the stores and restaurants are which are close to the school. If there are grocery stores and some restaurants near the school, this will be helpful so that community-based instruction will include stores which are close by. By utilizing stores that are near the school, the teacher can also have students learn to cross streets. Street crossing is a very important part of community-based instruction.

For variety, different stores and restaurants should be included in the weekly or bi-weekly schedule so that students will be exposed to a variety of community sites. Even if only two grocery stores and two different restaurants are available in the neighborhood, they can be scheduled in a variety of sequences so the students will encounter differences among the areas in which they shop and buy their food. It will not be possible to continually add stores and restaurants, but if at least some grocery stores and restaurants are added to the experience, each store and restaurant will hopefully have something new to teach the student. For example, in some restaurants the people order at a counter while at other restaurants the students wait at their tables until a waiter or waitress takes the student's order. Students with disabilities need the practice ordering in both these types of restaurants.

Additionally, when scheduling community-based instruction it is necessary to take no more than one or two students with disabilities into the community with their trainers and or staff. According to Brown (1991) if more than one or two students with disabilities are in the community at one time they will appear too obtrusive and will bring attention to themselves and this situation is not encouraged. Too often, according to (Brown 1991), we go against the law of natural proportion (more than one or two persons with disabilities are in one place) and thus bring attention to the students with disabilities who are in the community. People who are standing near the students with disabilities will not ignore their presence if there are several students, and, passersby may stop and ask questions about the training that is taking place in the community. It has been this writer's experience that students with disabilities, especially those who have autism or other severe behavior difficulties, will be obtrusive if more than one student is shopping or is eating in a restaurant. Also, if the store and restaurant personnel are not used to having people with disabilities in their facilities they may be distracted by having students with severe disabilities in their stores and restaurants.

LIABILITY

Liability is a very major concern for teachers, administrators, parents, and anyone who works closely with students out in the community. Because students are participating in many activities related to their individualized education plan, the schools will bear liability whenever a student is injured while participating in community-based instruction. The school is responsible for all activities the students are involved in, both at school and on the student's way to, from, or at, a community training site.

This writer coordinated a community-based program at a university in the Southwest and she became aware that liability for students' actions also had to be covered during community-based training, whenever a student was injured either at the university or on the student's way to and from the training site. The students and teachers must be covered in the same way when they are on field trips or in their classrooms; in this example, the community becomes the classroom. Permission slips must be completed by the parents and/or guardians and they must be filed by the teachers. The permission slip should be in the student's native or home language so that parents and or guardians whose first language is not English can complete the slip. According to an attorney this writer worked closely with on her university/based project with adults in the community, the permission slip will not protect the school personnel against liability claims if there is negligence on the school's part, but it does help parents feel that someone is assuming responsibility in case something were to happen to the students while they and the teachers and staff are in the community.

The best thing to do when developing a permission slip for community-based training which parents will sign is to consult with the school's legal advisor or lawyer. Most of them will be informed in terms of overall guidelines of liability and will also be helpful in explaining how the liability coverage works on those documents.

As transition director for the project this writer relied heavily on legal advice from the lawyer in the system and one who understood public school law as it applied to students with disabilities.

If the proper student/staff ratio is maintained, then the likelihood of something going wrong is lessened considerably.

Many automobile insurance companies do not cover the students or other people when it comes to their being transported in automobiles of the staff or parents. The two school districts where this writer did consulting work in the area of community-based instruction wanted the students to ride the school bus or city transportation or city bus whenever the community-based instruction involved training students in malls, shops, or worksites away from the school site. The school districts where this writer worked as a consultant for community-based instruction also stressed that teachers and staff should strive to identify other training sites within walking distance of the school and use them whenever possible.

When natural sites are established for students within walking distance of the schools, the students can also learn to walk and cross streets safely. Teaching them to look to the right and turn to the left to check for oncoming cars can be helpful when crossing busy as well as less busy streets and intersections.

When students are transported on school buses, parents have an opportunity to participate on the trip with some of the children, and in learning about community-based instruction become more supportive of the entire process.

This writer noted in working with Latino parents in the Southwest that because they really wanted their sons/daughters to read and write, they often did not support training their children in the community. By allowing parents to be part of the process and learn what was involved in going shopping, crossing streets, etc. many Latino parents started to be more supportive of the training their sons/daughters were experiencing in the community.

Another consideration that needs to be thought about carefully is taking precautions so that if students become separated or lost momentarily they can be found and assisted. What is helpful is attaching a laminated identification card to the students' community training notebook. The card should have the student's name address, phone number, and social security number if the student is older, and the name and phone number of the school or program where the student participates. Again if the student's first language is English and/or if the student lives in a community where another language is most often spoken, it is important to also put that information in the language that is most often spoken in the community where the students are shopping or are eating. Several times in the university adult program in the Southwest which is so near Mexico, many of the people in the downtown area spoke Spanish only and had little awareness of English; when they came across students who may have wandered momentarily from the other students, they would speak to the students in Spanish. Many of the students could understand, because they knew Spanish and were able to cue or point to their notebook. Then the community people looked in the student's notebooks, read the Spanish, and were able to make the appropriate telephone call or take the student to a place where he/she could be connected to the group once again.

The identification card should not only consider majority languages spoken in the community but should also have medical information about the student. For example, if the student is on medication or has epilepsy or another serious condition, such information is vital.

BUDGET OR FISCAL CONSIDERATIONS

Community-based instruction will require funds for paying for the use of the school or city bus, paying for some of the student's food, and covering other incidentals that may come along. For example, giving the students a small amount of money to purchase a fruit or soft drinks so they can have the opportunity to learn how to buy items at the store or restaurant is an excellent training technique. Many children and/or adults come from rural and urban settings where the parents and or guardians are unable to give them money to buy food or make a purchase at the store. Some of the children would miss some opportunities to practice such functional skills if some money was not made available through creative means periodically.

Teachers and staff this writer worked closely with in the Southwest usually asked the P.T.A., Parent Teacher, or other community organizations to assist them with funds so that all students would have the opportunity to participate fully in community-based instruction. In other instances, many of the teachers, along with this writer, applied for and received some small grants, or spoke to various community organizations in order to obtain funds for students whose parents were not working or could not afford to give them food and spending money so they could fully participate in the training.

Some schools would often pack lunches for the students so they could eat food while out in the community, thus reducing the need for supplemental funds. If teachers work closely with the principals and parent/ teacher associations, many creative possibilities can be found to assist students to participate as completely and fully as possible while out in the community.

It takes much hard work to find money sources in the community, but it can be done. Once some of the contacts are made, many foundations as well as other community organizations will continue to assist the teachers so that students in the program can participate more fully in community-based instruction.

Some teachers have often asked this writer what they need to do in order to write a small grant in order to secure funding from foundations or other community groups.

The best thing to do is to check with the particular foundation or community agency, who will give guidelines to apply for funds. Basically, foundations want some of the following:

1) Purpose of the program.
2) Description of the program.
3) Definition of terms such as community-based instruction.
4) Budget and budget explanations.
5) Letters of support (from parents, university officials, and/or school officials).

All points should be explained carefully and in detail, because a group of community people along with foundation staff will review the grant proposal, and they must have all explained clearly; otherwise they may not fund the school or community program seeking financial help not from hardness of heart, but from lack of understanding. The grant proposal must also explain that the program does not receive other funds (if this is indeed the case) so that the people reviewing the grant do not think that the school or university is taking funds from their budgets for this instruction.

CULTURAL AND LINGUISTIC CONSIDERATIONS

It is important not only to look at the budget, staff, liability, etc., but it is important to note the family environment, values, beliefs, and home or native language of the child.

A home survey or interview with the parents will help the very responses of the above considerations. A home survey might ask the following questions:

1) What language is spoken at home?
   ¿Cúal lenguaje se habla en la casa?
2) Who talks to your son or daughter the most?
   Quién habla más con sus hijos?
     Mother (Madre)
     Father (Padre)
     Brothers/Sisters (Hermanos y Hermanas)
   What language does the student hear most of the time at home?
   ¿Cúal es el lenguaje que oyen más frecuentemente sus hijos en la casa?
3) Do you know what community-based instruction means?
   ¿Sabe lo que quiere decir instrucción basada en la comunidad?
4) Do you know how many times your son or daughter will be going out to the community?
   ¿Sabe cuantas veses sus hijos van a salir a hacer el entrenamiento en la comunidad?
5) What is transition?
   ¿Qué quiere decir la palabra transción?
6) Do you see any reason why your son and or daughter cannot participate in the community-based training?
   ¿Existe algún problema por el cual su hijo/hija no puede participar en el programa de la comunidad?

Many Latino families initially do not want their sons/daughters to participate in community-based training because they feel they do not have to learn such things as shopping, crossing streets, or eating in a restaurant. It has always been stressed in many such families that learning to read and write will assist students to get ahead and be able to earn money and help the family out financially or become self supporting. It is a very new idea to have students use the community to learn from.

Further, many parents also fear that the children or young adults will not be able to take care of themselves if placed in the world outside their homes or school. Thus they cannot see the need for their sons/daughters to be training in a world which may not understand them or their disability.

It has been the experience of this writer that communication in the native or home language of the parents/children must be used to explain terms, concepts, and ideas of community-based instruction to the parents. Visual information, such as slides or photographs of the students participating in the community, must be made available to the parents. Training must be done more than once in small groups. The small groups allow the parents/guardians to feel free to talk and ask questions. Another Latino (or parent of whatever cultural group(s) the staff are working with) can help the staff facilitate the instruction to other parents.

By utilizing other parents, the parents who are in doubt can be better assisted and convinced of the value of the programming better then a teacher or other professional might be able to do.

Confianza or trust is a highly important concept and or belief to Latino parents. If they develop *confianza* or trust in teachers, principals or other peers, they will be better prepared to accept the words or ideas which that staff person or professional is trying to convey. Developing *confianza* or trust may take several months or even years to develop. It is something that comes through time and constant communication with the parents. Additionally *confianza* is developed when the parent/guardian sees that the learning the child or young adult and or adult is receiving is appropriate, and that the student is valued by the teacher and/or care providers.

Latino parents value "goodness" (Taylor Gibbs, 1991) or "una buena persona" more than some of the terms or jargon a professional may use with those parents. If the Latino parents see that Mr. Smith or Mrs. Jones or Señora Alvarez "es una buena persona," they will be more inclined to assist the teacher or support the teacher with the various goals the teachers may want to accomplish for their sons/daughters.

Latino people are also highly religious in many instances, and many rely on God to guide their wisdom and decision making concerning their children as well as their family lives. If they feel within their hearts that God is communicating to them that their child should not do a certain activity, they will often keep the children at home or will not allow the child to be involved in community based instruction.

Teachers should attempt to be patient and not criticize parents who they feel that religion is dictating to them what they should or should not do about their child. Communicating what the teacher is attempting to do for the child, emphasizing what the training should do for the child, and explaining how this will help the children presently and in the future will help some parents who are slow to accept new information about their son and/or daughter. Each parent is an individual, and the amount of explanation or time it might take him/her to understand more fully what the teacher is attempting to do will vary from family to family. The key lies in discovering each family's uniqueness and remembering that communication and patience are important keys in working with Latino parents.

It is always important to use an interpreter to assist the teacher who does not speak the home language of the family. An interpreter can be a family member or someone from the school or community. Latino families are impressed with the teachers or service providers who go to the child's home, or who care enough to take time to know more about the child. This is one of the ways "confianza" is developed. Once established, confianza is not easily destroyed unless something occurs between home and school which has not been communicated or carefully talked about before it was done or attempted with the child.

Thus community-based instruction, like all other aspects of teaching and training a child or young adult or adult, involves looking carefully at the child's environmental needs such as those things already discussed (liability, money considerations, etc.), and further it involves looking closely at the child's culture, language and beliefs. These are very important considerations when teaching children, and especially teaching children who come from second language backgrounds.

REFERENCES

Brown, L. (1991). Keynote Speaker, Supported Life Conference, Red Lion Inn, Sacramento, CA.

Durán, E. (1988). *Teaching the Moderately and Severely Handicapped Student and Autistic Adolescent.* Springfield, IL: Charles C Thomas.

Ford, A. & P. Miranda (1984). Community instruction: A natural cue and corrections decision model, *Journal of the Association for Persons with Severe Handicaps,* Vol. 9, No. 2, pp. 79–88.

Gaylord-Ross, R. et al. (1987). Community-referenced instruction in technological work. *Journal of Exceptional Children,* vol. 54, No. 2, pp. 112–120.

Gibbs, J. T. & L. N. Huang (1989). *Children of Color Psychological Interventions with Minority Youth,* San Francisco: Jossey-Bass.

Marger, M. N. (1991). *Race and ethnic relations: American and global perspectives* (2nd edition). St. Louis: Wadsworth., pp. 139–215.

Nietupski, J. et al. (1986). Guidelines for making simulation an effective adjunct to In Vivo community instruction. *Journal of the Association for Persons with Severe Handicaps.* Vol. II, No. 1, pp. 12–18.

Powell, G. J. (1983). *The psychosocial development of minority group children.* New York: Brunner/Mazel, pp. 194–215.

Powell, G. J. (1983). *The psychosocial development of minority group children.* New York: Brunner/Mazel, pp. 77–114.

Sasso, G. (1988). The social effects of integration on non-handicapped children. *Education and Training in Mental Retardation.* Vol. 23, No. 1, pp. 18–23.

Rainforth, B. & J. York (1987). Integrating related services in community instruction, *Journal of the Association for Persons with Severe Handicaps,* Vol. 12, No. 3, pp. 190–198.

Solano County Superintendent of Schools, (1988). *Community-Based Instruction Policy and Procedures Handbook.*

Chapter Five

THE ADOLESCENT STUDENT WITH AUTISM

This chapter will define autism and will give characteristics of autism. Additionally, this chapter will note some programming considerations that must be made when placing students for training and work on the job site.

Many of the experiences shared in this chapter come directly from the writer, who has directed autism programs in the Southwest community in the public schools and in the University community. It was exciting to write this chapter, because there are so many of my students with autism who have taught me so many things through the years; indeed, my students have been my best teachers throughout the years.

Also, it was a good feeling to write this chapter because much more needs to be done to educate the teacher who will teach these students and similar students who have bizarre and self destructive characteristics. This writer can recall when she started to work directly over twelve years ago with parents and their young children who had autism. At first there was fear because this writer thought how little she knew about these children who exhibited such bizarre characteristics. Now, years later, this writer realizes that no other groups of students have taught her so much and has given her such opportunity, time and time again, to explore so many different approaches and techniques to work with these students.

DEFINITION OF AUTISM

Autism is a developmental disability which appears from birth through thirty months of age. It has also been defined by the American Psychiatric Association (1980) as a pervasive developmental disorder (not a psychosis) that has to be identified by thirty months of age (Jenson 1985). The term "infantile" is the name of the condition, emphasizing the fact that this condition is manifested during the early years of a child's life. The term autism also means "alone" or "separate." It was Leo Kanner, a child psychiatrist, who in 1943, first described the condition. The aloneness or separateness is very important to the condition. Students with autism demonstrate many ways of not relating to others. Some of this nonrelatedness appears in the children as they gaze and avoid having eye contact with other people. They also demonstrate this aloneness characteristic, which is most important to the definition, as seen in not allowing people to touch or hold them. They also have few play skills and no friendships.

Some additional characteristics which are a great part of the definition show autistic children as being stubborn or non-compliant; many resist changes. These changes could be temporary, minimal, and even of the slightest origin, but the students with autism will become extremely upset and almost bizarre-like because they are aware of the changes which are in the environment.

Students with autism lack social skills, and this is one of the major reasons their bizarre behaviors stand out even more, because they are unable to be around or relate to others in ways that are similar to students that are considered developmentally normal. The social skill development aspect is a continual life-long skill that must be planned for and carefully worked out so, that some improvement can be made in this area.

Another characteristic of autism is that many of the students do not have language skills. Twenty percent of the students with autism are mute. Many repeat things that teachers, parents, and or other students will tell them and this characteristic is referred to as "echolalia." According to Lovaas (1981), echolalia often indicates that students possessing this characteristic are capable of developing more language than many of us believe they are capable of learning.

Students with autism also have self-stimulatory behaviors. They will do things over and over or gaze at objects in the environment as part of their self-stimulatory behaviors. Students with autism will rock, spin, and hand flap. They enjoy engaging in these behaviors, which often are exhibited in different degrees from childhood to adult.

Students with autism often exhibit another characteristic which sets them apart from other students who may just be mentally retarded. The characteristic they also exhibit is called "overselectivity," in which they learn new skills but attend to only a limited set of stimuli from the environment, or to irrelevant stimuli (Lovaas, Koegel, & Schreibman, 1979). This characteristic interferes with learning in a number of ways. For example, if a teacher names an object and then tries to get an autistic child to choose between two objects (one which is the object named), the child might respond to the object the teacher glances at (irrelevant cue) instead of responding to the object's name. Schreibman and Lovaas (1973) found that autistic students knew how to discriminate between male and female dolls but when the doll's shoes were changed the students with autism selected the shoes to focus their attention on, and the students could no longer identify which was the male and which was the female. This characteristic, along with the others, have to be attended to by the teacher and parents when teaching the student with autism.

Other characteristics of the autistic student include the following:

1) The student with autism resists being touched or held.
2) The student with autism does not imitate other children at play.
3) The student with autism does not follow simple commands.
4) The student with autism is very involved with rituals.
5) The student with autism "looks through people."
6) The student with autism plays with inanimate objects.
7) The student with autism does not wait for needs to be met (wants things immediately).
8) The student with autism has no social smile.
9) The student with autism has difficulty with pronouns.

During preschool through elementary years many of these behaviors become more pronounced.

As the student gets older and passes adolescence (during the time the body is undergoing many changes), many of these behaviors or characteristics become pronounced. It is important for teachers, careproviders, and parents to realize that after the students pass puberty they exhibit fewer of the characteristics such as tantruming, self abuse, and other inflexible behaviors. Part of the reason for such changes in the students' behavior is that the body of the autistic student has become more stable, and fewer changes are occurring in the student as rapidly as were exhibited earlier.

Thus the most difficult times to teach these students are during their early years when the students are learning languages and how to follow directions, and the second period during their adolescent years.

PREVOCATIONAL ACTIVITIES

Having younger students with autism who are learning to say a few words or are learning to respond to a few simple directions is the beginning of prevocational activities.

As early as five or six years of age, students can begin activities designed to teach them to work and complete tasks on a job in their teen years.

In the special education program which this writer organized and conducted with her college students at the University of Texas at El Paso for eleven years, many ideas were generated by means of teachers, parents, and caregivers working and discussing together.

Some of the activities included first teaching the students to attend and to pay attention. This is done in language training and play activities that the student is engaging with the teacher. This writer has noticed the difference between students in later years if they are taught to attend to the trainer and or careproviders and those who have not learned to attend.

One of the first persons to experience success teaching autistic students to attend was Ivar Lovaas (1981). Lovaas experienced major success with severely disabled students with autism by teaching them to look on command at the teacher. For example, the student was taught to sit in a chair with feet down on the floor and hands quietly on the child's legs or lap; when this position was achieved, the teacher almost instantly said, "Look at me." This was repeated for several minutes. And each time the child followed the teacher's oral command of "Look at me" (keeping his/her feet on the floor and hands resting quietly on his/her lap) the child was praised for looking at the teacher. The teacher recorded the number of times the student followed the teacher's directions and looked at the teacher. This writer observed Dr. Lovaas demonstrating this attending instruction with several very severe students with autism and was impressed to see how they could learn many other activities after the compliance training.

This writer took some of this similar training to her community in the Southwest and discovered that with consistency the students continued to make progress if the technique was used on a daily basis. Within weeks the students progressed to learn other skills because they were listening to different people telling them, "Look at me" and then giving them oral directions. Almost immediately this training needs to be presented to the students in other environments, such as in the student's home, playground, and various community area where this student could generalize to his/her environments. This allows the student with autism to generalize or transfer learning to other environments otherwise learning becomes situation specific. Until attending is taught the autistic student will make little progress in all other skills.

As the students become older, if they have not learned to attend because they had no training when they were younger, then it is still imperative to teach them to look at whoever is speaking to them or giving them directions. Before the student begins training in his/her vocational task, the trainer can say, "Are you ready to work?" "Look at what you are going to do." "Get ready." After a couple of weeks of telling the student, "Are you ready to work? The autistic student is better able to learn his/her work. Again generalizing can be taught to the older student in order that he/she can transfer such skills to other environments.

Once again, failing to teach a student to attend when he/she is older and is already on-the-job training will not allow the student to be successful; such neglect on the part of the teacher will cause the student to lose his/her training site, because he/she will not be able to focus on his/her work.

Other prevocational skills which need to be taught to younger students with autism include teaching them to communicate and or request items, stay on task without self-stemming or engaging in self-abusive behavior, working on fine and gross motor areas, teaching the student not to engage in ritualistic behaviors, and seeing what other skills the. student needs as he/she is in the work environment. These goals can be accomplished by carefully working with the student and observing daily as the student engages in a variety of activities. Additional prevocational activities that make for excellent pre-job training include planning activities to develop rate, duration, and accuracy.

COMMUNICATION AND OR GESTURING INSTRUCTION

Before the student can work, the student will need to be able to request his/her needs and desires in whatever environment he/she is. For instance if the student cannot turn on a faucet to wash dishes or find the detergent to put in the wash bin, then the student will not be able to successfully complete his/her work. Thus it is necessary to observe and assess what communication skills the student has before beginning a vocational program for the student. Teachers and/or trainers often overlook checking the student's ability to convey or request his/her desires. Thus when the student proceeds to work he/she does not complete tasks, etc., simply because he/she is unable to communicate. It is a well known fact that students with autism often tantrum severely because they feel frustration because they are unable to communicate their desires to others. Teachers should have a checklist of important words they need to teach students before they go out into the community. Words like "bathroom," "men," "women," "water," "food," "bus," "home," "money," "name," "address," are a few important words students need to learn to recognize and learn so they can better communicate their desires. Other important words would be words from work and the community that are encountered by the student daily.

Periodically the trainer and or teacher needs to decide if the students have learned the words or have not learned the words; if the latter, they need to continue getting practice on the words. It is important to keep on teaching these word recognition to continue teaching. Many students with autism have poor short term memories (Lovaas, 1981), thus the added exposure to the words is necessary.

Photographs, gestures, and/or signs (American sign language or manual educational signs) can be taught to the student who is non-verbal so he/she can learn to communicate. Discovering several means to teach communication may be appropriate for the students in order for them to communicate their needs and desires.

As the students get older, the best way to teach them to learn language and or communication is to teach words in a variety of environments, and not teach language or communication in one single place or in a formal setting or manner. Such techniques were likely done with the child earlier, and it is not necessary for the same methods to be use when the student is older. Learning to communicate is done more effectively in various functional environments, and as often as is needed by the student.

COMPLIANCE TRAINING

It was mentioned earlier that the student needs to learn to attend and follow directions as a basic part of learning to work.

Such compliance training that can be very useful is following a program such as Core Management by (William Jenson (1985). The Core Management Program consists of Parts I–IV: Part I of the program is entitled "Get Ready"; Part II is "Following Directions"; Part III is "Visual Tracking"; and Part IV is "Peer Tutoring."

In Part I, "Get Ready," the student is taught to tap feet firmly on the floor with hands down on lap. This is done on command as teacher firmly says, "Get Ready," and claps his/her hands. This should be done for approximately ten minutes in the morning and ten minutes in the afternoon initially. Doing this exercise early in the training for twenty minutes daily will help the student to learn that someone is in "control" of the student, or that the student is expected to follow directions when various people give the student commands. It is important to give a firm, crisp "Get Ready." The voice should be firm because this quality establishes that the teacher or careprovider is the "boss" or is in command. Many teachers who have never used compliance training believe that if they do the training with the student only when the student misbehaves, then the compliance training will be effective. Such is not the case. The students do not improve if the training is used only when the student acts inappropriately. (The teacher or trainer should clap his/her hands firmly as the command of "Get Ready" is given to the student.) When the student is older, he/she may be harder to manage than a younger student with autism especially if compliance training has not been provided earlier it may be necessary to simply say firmly, "Get Ready." Also using the firm hand clap to bring the student to reality and out of a daze is also effective. Again, using this strategy on a daily basis for twenty minutes a day will be helpful in establishing compliance among the adolescents with autism. If this is done consistently the student will learn to follow directions during vocational training and on-the-job training. Without this voice control the student will be less able to complete tasks as he/she reaches adolescence.

The second part of the compliance training program is "Following Directions." In "Following Directions" the student is told by the teacher to "Come here" and later is told to "Come here please." The trainer or teacher should have the student come to the teacher each time he/she calls the student. A plus ("+") is recorded each time the student comes to the teacher as the student was commanded. Each time the student complies with the teacher's directions the student is allowed to move slightly further from the teacher. This idea of having the student move slightly farther from the teacher each time the student follows the command of "Come here" should teach the student that he/she can handle more and more freedom. If the student fails to comply with the "Come Here" command he/she should be moved closer to the teacher or trainer each time. "Close" may mean that the student gets an arm's length from the teacher. In this manner or position the teacher can reach the student quickly if he/she is not being compliant. Thus, the student learns that he/she can not run away from the teacher.

Part III of the Compliance Training Program is "Visual Tracking." In visual tracking the teacher first has the student sit down in a "Get ready" position. The teacher then sits across the student and gives the command, "Get ready." After the student is attending and is looking at the teacher the teacher now says, "What's that?" (Holding an object in front of the student). The objective of the visual tracking is to get the student to look at the object on command. After this step the teacher holds a second object and says to the student, "What's that?" This procedure continues until ten objects are shown to the student and the student has looked at least nine of the objects. This procedure, like the previous two steps, are critical in teaching the student to comply. Visual tracking should be done in other environments and with different trainers. Such training in other environments will help the student generalize to other environments within and this variety of situation is helpful in tracking the students to do the same task in a variety of places.

Part IV of the Compliance Training program is entitled "Peer Tutoring." In Peer Tutoring other students in the class attempt to do the various parts (I–III) of the program so that the student will be able to comply following peer student directions. This procedure once again becomes extremely helpful when the student is out in the community and is receiving directions from a variety of people. This variety will be helpful to them and the trainers and or teachers as training progresses with the student.

Students with autism find it especially difficult to be flexible to any change in their routine. If such strategies are employed early, when the student is younger, as the student reaches adolescence and adulthood the student may have less difficulty complying with various trainers.

Other prevocational activities for students with autism include providing opportunities for the student to learn rate, duration, and accuracy.

Rate, duration, and accuracy are some of the very skills that some teachers consider important to teach students as they are getting ready to learn to do various tasks. (These terms are defined below.) These skills become even more important for the trainer to know when the student begins to do vocational training and or becomes employed.

Rate is defined as "speed." Speed is important to teach the student, because if the student cannot keep up with the normal peers in class, or with normal people out in the community or at work, then the student will not stay on the job nor be able to perform other skills that require the student to complete work at a certain speed. Teachers can have the student perform a variety of activities to teach *rate* or *speed*. For example, the teacher can have the students perform various tasks and the students can be timed. The students should be praised. When they complete certain tasks at the speed or rate that normal developing students should complete. If the student is washing dishes, the task can be timed. If the student is progressing nicely on this task, the teacher can say, "Good working fast."

A chart of the student's progress will be helpful to keep so that everyone involved will know how he/she is progressing. The student should be shown the chart so that he/she can see if any improvement is being made. This chart becomes motivating to some students, and in many instances they will try harder on any other task which is timed. The chart and the praise will be helpful in showing students how they are performing and will encourage them to try to improve on their next timed test.

Duration is another work skill which we have to teach students when they are younger so that once they are working on a job they will be able to stay on task for longer periods of time. Duration or staying on the job for longer periods of time is a difficult accomplishment at first, especially if the students have not done much vocational training at the beginning or have severe tantruming behaviors.

It has been the experience of this writer that many students with autism can begin working for five to ten minutes at a time, and gradually the length of time on the job can be increased considerably. The time that the student works or stays on task gradually increases for students as students are given more time to work. This writer had a student with autism who started training at the age of twelve and could work only ten minutes at a time without tantruming and/or engaging in inappropriate behavior. At the end of a four-year period, and after gradually allowing the student to train for an hour to two hours daily, the student was able to work without engaging in inappropriate behaviors for as much as half a day.

Teachers should discover jobs that students can do around the classroom or in the school or community environment, and allow them to work and increase their time on their work or task gradually. The gradual increase of time on the job will help develop the student's endurance. Endurance can be measurably increased in students with autism, especially if charts and records are maintained to see if the student's duration or time on task is gradually increasing.

Another important area that students with autism should be encouraged to accomplish is *accuracy*. In accuracy the trainer is concerned with making certain that the steps to the job are accomplished as was originally intended. Accuracy can be checked as the student completes or does not complete each of the steps in the task. (Accuracy can be checked for instance, as managers on-the-job or teachers check to see if students have for instance completed each of the steps of the task, based on standards set by the person who is most familiar with how the job should be completed, and the acceptable rate of performance. But achieving or completing each step in order is of primary importance in checking accuracy).

The student with autism has a tendency to fixate (to look at an object for a long period of time), a characteristic that can be undesirable but it does enable such a student to concentrate on task, if the concentration does not go too fast and become an act of fixation. Again this is a skill which gradually improves as the student is given correction-feedback as he/she completes his/her work. Managers of the various sites often noted that students with autism were attentive to their job because of their ability to fixate on work they were completing. Students with autism are not easily distracted and again this makes for attentiveness and not making errors on their job especially when they are actively engaged on a particular task.

JOBS AND JOB TRAINING FOR STUDENTS WITH AUTISM

We have now seen what we need to track students with autism as we train them to become better prepared to handle their jobs and/or do vocational training. We will now look at some jobs and job training that students will autism can perform.

It has been the experience of this writer that once students with autism receive training to do jobs successfully in the community at an early age (eleven or younger) for a few hours a day, then they are going to be able to accomplish more work once they are placed in their jobs for pay.

The key is giving them enough time on the vocational training phase and slowly increase the hours and/or days to the point that they can do more of the training.

Some of the jobs that this writer has found useful to track their various skills have been food service; motel, janitorial, or office work; working in a convalescent home; and sorting catalogues in a travel agency. Within food service, for example, the students could load and unload dishwashers, stack clean dishes, sort silverware, wash and package potatoes for baking to be eaten by students and faculty, vacuum various floor areas, and do any other task which can be determined by looking at the various jobs in the food service area.

Students should be rotated on the various jobs at least every four months. This rotation gives the students opportunities to learn to do a variety of jobs. This variety also gives students with autism an opportunity to see what work they like best, and they are also able to see what they perform best at.

In many of the places where the students are doing their job training, employers often hire the student with autism if the student has shown himself/herself to be a good worker. In the program this writer directed in the Southwest many of the employers hired the students. This result was especially true of students who had been training with them for more than a year. One of the most popular job sites for the students was the fast food restaurant. The students did well where there were jobs or tasks that allowed the trainee to complete tasks which were repetitive. Many students became gainfully employed in such establishments as Pizza Hut, Taco Bell, and Whataburger. Here the students would do such tasks as opening crates or boxes where the lettuce and other materials were packaged. Also, the students loaded the dishwasher and stacked trays or dishes that were used in preparing the various fast foods. Fast food restaurants also employ more people with disabilities because many of these restaurants hire college students on a part time basis; and there is always room to have people complete the jobs college students vacate. Further, fast food restaurants always have periods in the early morning (7:00 to 11:00 p.m.) where they cannot find people to work. Once again this opportunity for work training becomes ideal for students with autism, because many of them need to work and remain actively involved in some useful endeavor.

As the students are working or training it is a good idea to keep a chart on the different jobs each student has trained in or has obtained for pay. This record will give the trainer or teacher a summary of the student's activity. Also, it will note for the trainers how many different jobs or training sites the student has had. This charting is especially helpful when several students are under one teacher's care.

CO-WORKERS

Co-workers need to know about autism so that they will be supportive of the students who are placed in their job site. Too often co-workers who are not aware of autism and the behaviors which can result from having workers with autism around the job site will be unsupportive, especially if students with autism exhibit noncompliant or tantruming behaviors. A short workshop should be given to employees to show them what autism is. An outline of a proposed workshop that could be given to various co-workers follows: (See Figure 10).

FIGURE 10
Autism Workshop Outline

I.   Autism — Prevalence

II.   What is Autism? (Show some slides)

III.   Characteristics of Autism

IV.   Working Alongside a Student with Autism

V.   How Can I Help Student with Autism in Worksite?

VI.   Questions and Answers

When opportunity has been provided for the co-workers to learn more about the condition of autism, co-workers are generally more supportive of the trainee because they understand more of what the condition involves.

It has been this writer's experience that fewer problems occurred in the job sites with co-workers and the students with autism when the workshop was given and later follow-up was provided with a staff person continuing to come to the job site and check to see if any problems arose as the students were receiving training. The extra mile that was taken with co-workers helped students stay on their jobs, because many were given the support from co-workers that comes only after co-workers had a better understanding of the condition. In sites where the co-workers did not receive training about autism, the co-workers were often afraid of the students who became non-compliant or who tantrumed. A few of the co-workers complained to the managers of the employment sites, and as a result some of the students with autism lost their jobs. Wehman (1981) reports that co-workers are a major key to the success of a person with disabilities staying on the work force. This writer would add that for students with autism, especially, it is very necessary to share with co-workers what autism is and how they can help their co-workers be successful on their jobs.

FOLLOW-UP AND EVALUATION

No program is complete unless we know what works or does not work with our students.

Once again, follow-up will tell the teacher what areas in the training or employment were effective or not effective. Also follow-up will tell the teacher or trainer which students have been successful on the job and which students have had to be moved from one job site to another.

According to Wehman (1981), students should be followed or checked on their jobs for up to five years. It has been this writer's experience that it takes up to a year for a student to begin feeling like he/she is comfortable on his job, and another year to begin developing some social skills on the job.

Follow-up also lets staff of vocational training programs of students with autism evaluate some of the following:

1) Were the pretraining activities are useful with the students?
2) Was compliance training effective?
3) Did starting at an early age help the student stay on the job?

Evaluating the overall effectiveness of the program is necessary in order to see if the entire vocational training and job placement is effective. This evaluation should be done at least yearly, because too often if no evaluation is done of the program many students do not make the progress needed for staying permanently on jobs. (Also, if no evaluation of the entire program is done we will not discover how many are being paid or are not being paid for their work.)

Evaluation of the program should also reveal the parents' thoughts on the overall training and placement of their sons/daughters in the training program. Parents provide an insight to specific reasons why their son and/or daughter is not performing to capacity or suggest how their sons/daughters can do better in their training. The more parents are involved in giving feedback, suggestions, and information to the teacher, trainer, or staff, the stronger will be the communication between the parents and staff and the program will be stronger.

Parents of students with autism often go through much stress, because they have many concerns about their child's behavior, and his/her long-term success on the job. Often they need support and the listening ear of the staff, because many parents need to ventilate and share their heavy hearts with someone who will listen and understand. Too often parents are too close to their own children or situation to be objective, or to see what the problem with their son and or daughter may actually be. By talking to a staff person who is working closely with their son and or daughter, insight can come into the education and/or training of the child.

Thus evaluating and follow-up reveal many important components of the program, such as the employment and training of students. Without starting the training early, including pretraining activities education, and involving parents in the program, quite often students will not make progress and will also not stay on jobs permanently.

THE CULTURALLY AND LINGUISTICALLY DIFFERENT STUDENT WITH AUTISM

By the year 2000 there will be many minority students in our schools. In many cases these "minority" students will comprise an actual majority in our communities as well as our classes.

This writer has worked for many years in the Southwest, where the majority of students who attend classes are Latino. Latino students are defined as Mexicans and all those who have roots in Latin American countries. The term "Latino" is the term most frequently used to describe Hispanic students.

Many of the students with autism whom this coordinator worked with were from Mexican and Mexican-American backgrounds. As a result of their roots, many of the students knew either Spanish or Spanish and English. It is important to realize that if the students knew one language that they have an opportunity to hear a short summary of their home or first language as part of their instruction in the classroom. Thus previewing the lesson or concept for the student in their native language before switching to English will be very helpful to get them to know the concept more thoroughly. For example, if the student is going to do a certain task in his job the teacher will say, *"Vas a hacer tu trabajo."* (You are going to do your job). *En primer lugar, vas a limpiar las mesas.* (First of all you will clean the tables). *En segundo lugar, vas a poner los materiales sobre la mesa.* (Secondly you are going to put all of the materials on the table). After this brief synopsis or summary the student will get the same information in English. This procedure will continue until the student begins to complete the task and does not seem to have any further questions. The previewing approach is from ESL or English as a Second Language methodology, and has been shown to be most effective with second language learners.

Other important things that need to be considered when teaching students of other cultures include the teacher's knowing some of the family needs and values of the student. Some questions this writer has found helpful in the Southwest in working with Latino families who have students with autism include some of the following:

1) How many brothers and sisters are in the student's family?
2) What do mother and father do?
3) What are the family's hopes and dreams concerning their son and or daughter with autism?
4) How do they feel about their son and or daughter working? And/or working for pay?
5) What is the main language spoken at home? Who speaks what language to the child? (brothers/sisters/mother/father?)
6) Do the children play with neighbor children and/or brothers and sisters at home? What language do they use at play?
7) Do the parents read to their children at home? In what language?

Taking time to discover answers to some of these questions is important, because it will give some insights into culture, language, and some of the beliefs of the family. Latino families in many cases have strong beliefs about a student and his/her potential to work. Many Latino parents believe, for example, that they will live forever and they do not feel their son and/or daughter should work or will ever need to work. Others believe that they as parents can provide for their son and or daughter. Because of the severity of the autism condition many parents especially believe that no one can look out for their son and or daughter as well as the family or parents could at home.

Other parents have strong views, for example on the type of management they will be doing with their son and/or daughter. Again this is an important consideration that needs to be explored with parents of persons with autism.

Latino parents can be strong advocates of a program, especially if they see how the program is helping their son and or daughter. The parents can also be unsupportive, especially if they do not see how they fit in with the program or do not see how the program is of help to their son and/or daughter. In such cases parents will lose trust or *confianza* in the teacher and/or program and they will not support the program or the teacher. *Confianza* (trust) is a most important component in the Latino culture, and it takes a while to develop this quality among parents of these populations. Parents do not trust just anyone. Trust must be built gradually and carefully. Once trust or *confianza* is established, the Latino parents and family will faithfully support the teacher and or program. If *confianza* is ever destroyed, it will be very hard to develop strong ties with the family once again.

Further, it has been suggested that knowing about the family's culture and values will strongly affect the program and thus the student. Many Latino parents are very religious, and, because religion is tied in closely with how parents feel about work and where their son and or daughter will live, it is imperative that staff members discover what the parents feel about their son and/or daughter working; also it is important to discover what the parents will do with their son and/or daughter once the child finishes school at age 21 or 22. Very often the views of the family cannot easily be changed nor can new ideas be added to what they already believe. The staff needs to assess the situation and lead the parents from whatever point where they are to a desired new understanding. To try to change parents' views too quickly, or to apply too much strength will not be helpful to the student or the program. Parents often begin to accept new views about their son and/or daughter, especially if they trust or have *confianza* in the professional.

Obviously, Latino families have their own cultural beliefs and values. These values affect what can or cannot be done with the student with autism. It is necessary to discover what can be done with the student with autism by working closely with the families of these students. The long range effects of spending time to discover about the students' families will provide a greater amount of understanding of all that a person needs to do with the students in class. Without such understanding, success may well be impossible.

REFERENCES

Carr, E. G. (1979). Teaching autistic children to use sign language: Some research issues. *Journal of Autism and Developmental Disorders*, Vol. 9, 345–359.

Durán, E. (1988). *Teaching a Moderately and Severely Handicapped Student and Autistic Adolescent with Particular Attention to Bilingual Special Education*. Springfield, IL: Charles C Thomas.

Jenson, W. R. & K. Reavis (1982). Autism Decision Matrix: Salt Lake City: Utah State Office of Education publication.

Jenson, W. R. et al., (1985). Autism Prescriptive Checklist and Interventions Manual. Salt Lake City: Utah State Office of Education publication.

Jenson, W. R. & CBTU Staff (1980). *Parent Training Curriculum for Families of Developmentally Disabled Children*. Salt Lake City: Governor's Council on Developmental Disabilities and Children's Behavior Therapy Unit publication.

Lovaas, I., R. Koegel & L. Schreibman (1979). Stimulus overselectivity in autism: A review of the research. *Psychological Bulletin*, Vol. 86, 1236–1254.

Lovaas, I. (1981). *Teaching Developmentally Disabled Children: The Me Book*, Baltimore: University Park Press.

Miramontes, O. B. (1991). Organizing for effective paraprofessional services in special education: a multilingual/multiethnic instructional service team model. *RASE (Remedial and Special Education)*, Vol 12 (1), 29–36.

Ritvo, E. R. & B. J. Freeman (1984). A medical model of autism: Etiology, pathology, and treatment, *Pediatric Annals*, Vol. 13, 298–305.

Rodríguez, J. R., S. B. Morgan & G. R. Geffken (1991). A comparative evaluation of adaptive behavior in children and adolescents with autism, *Journal of Autism and Developmental Disorders*, Vol. 21, No. 2, 1991, pp. 187–195.

Rojahn, J. & W. J. Helsel (1991). The aberrant behavior checklist with children and adolescents with dual diagnosis, *Journal of Autism and Developmental Disorders*, Vol. 21, No. 1, 1991, pp. 17–27.

Schreibman, L. & I. Lovaas (1973). Overselective response to social stimuli by autistic children. *Journal of Abnormal Child Psychology*, Vol. 1, 152–168.

Wehman, P. (1981). *Competitive Employment New Horizons for Severely Disabled Individuals*, Baltimore: Paul Brookes, pp. 1–236.

Chapter Six

SOCIAL ACCEPTANCE OF PERSONS WITH DISABILITIES AT EMPLOYMENT SETTINGS: ASSESSMENT AND INTERVENTION PROCEDURES

Hyun-Sook Park, Phyllis Tappe, Marlene Simon and Thom Wozniah

Job retention and job satisfaction are both measures of a successful job placement. Retention most often occurs when an individual exhibits job competence. This includes both responsibility and task production, and also social awareness, encompassing both task-related social skills and personal social skills (Greenspan & Shoultz, 1981; Brickery, Browning, & Campbell, 1982; Salzberg, Lignugaris/Kraft, & McCuller, 1988). The person's social awareness and related social skills can facilitate job retention by reducing some of the involuntary behaviors that are reason for termination (e.g., Greenspan & Shoultz, 1981). Further, these factors can enhance job satisfaction and the quality of work life by increasing social acceptance at the work site (French, Caplan, & Van Harrison, 1982; House, 1981). Social acceptance at work settings implies that a person is engaged in social interactions with other coworkers/supervisors and is able to develop a support relationship with them. Social acceptance has implication beyond the demonstration of just so-called appropriate social skills. It involves the use of social skills to develop mutually satisfying or reciprocal relationships with others (e.g., receiving and providing social support).

The establishment of the social acceptance of an employee with disabilities can be viewed as a dynamic part of interaction between two components: a person with disabilities and his/her environment (Rogers-Warren & Warren, 1977; Williams, 1977; Chadsey-Rusch, 1986). Figure 11 presents the conceptualization of social acceptance of a person with disabilities in the work setting. The first component—the person—includes the person's ability to initiate and maintain social interaction and social relationship. It usually requires the person to demonstrate the appropriate social skills and motivation to engage himself/herself in social interactions. The second component includes the physical, organizational, and social ecologies that may influence social interactions at work settings (Chadesy-Rusch and Rusch, 1988). Physical ecology refers to the actual physical settings which may influence social interactions of employees, for example, an arrangement of tables and chairs; some people may feel comfortable interacting with others when there are several small round tables rather than one big rectangular table. Organizational ecology refers to the policy, management style, and program factors that may affect social acceptance and social interactions. For example, if a supervisor believes in social integration of employees with disabilities and makes an effort to include these employees into social spheres of activity, the employees with disabilities are more likely to have opportunity to participate in the establishments of social acceptance. Social ecology refers to a receptor culture that non-disabled workers create, i.e., non-disabled co-workers' readiness/receptiveness to initiate and maintain social interaction and relationships with employees with disabilities. When non-disabled co-workers are more receptive to social interaction with employees with disabilities, it is more likely that a positive social interaction and relationship is established between the employees with disabilities and their non-disabled counterparts.

As shown in Figure 11, an employee's social acceptance depends on a good match between the person and the environment. Social acceptance will be deterred when employees do not possess adequate social repertoires, and when work environments do not promote acceptance of differences among disabled and non-disabled workers. A good social ecological match can reduce stress on the job by promoting good communication, enhancing relationships, and increasing understanding of workplace standards. It also helps establish a good social support system that can contribute to psychological well-being at the work setting and the quality of work life (e.g., French et al., 1982; House, 1981).

This interdependence between a person and the environment presents significant implications for assessment and intervention for social acceptance of an employee with disabilities at work settings—it emphasizes that both assessment and intervention need to focus not only on the individual, but also on the environment and the interaction between the two (Bronfenbrenner, 1979). However, traditional social intervention for persons with disabilities has addressed the person variable only, usually in terms of social skills training. Recently, Breen, Kennedy, and Haring (1991) attempted to define, assess, and intervene social relationship from

FIGURE 11
Conceptualization of Social Acceptance of an Employee with Disabilities

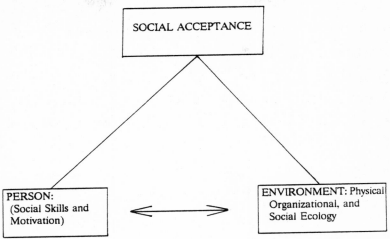

a broad perspective. That is, they incorporated social context (environment and other contextual variables) in their assessment and intervention on social inclusion of students with disabilities. With Breen et al. (1991) they mainly focus on school and community environments, their work can be well adopted into work settings. This chapter will discuss assessment and intervention procedures which will help teachers and employment specialists promote the social acceptance of persons with disabilities at work settings, e.g., social interaction and support relationships.

ASSESSMENT OF SOCIAL ACCEPTANCE

The assessment of social acceptance of persons with disabilities at work settings typically follows the conceptualization of social acceptance presented in Figure 11: person and environment. Therefore, the assessment procedure should include procedures directed to both person (social skill and motivation assessment) and environment (ecology assessment). Figure 12 presents a flow chart of the assessment procedure.

Initial Assessment

A teacher/employment specialist should conduct an initial screening in order to find out whether or not the person with disabilities maintains a good social acceptance and support relationships with other co-workers

FIGURE 12
An Assessment Procedure For Social Acceptance of an Employee with Disabilities

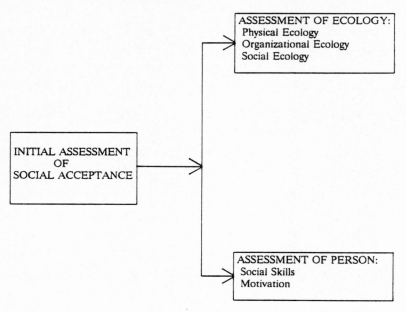

and also to evaluate the need for further assessments in specific areas such as social skills. This initial assessment may involve a survey with co-workers/supervisors using a checklist that includes items on general social interactions, support relationships, and perceptions toward an employee with disabilities. The items can be generated from inputs by co-workers/supervisors, or literature, ecological inventories, and observation of non-disabled workers' social interaction with each other.

Ecological inventories refers to a process that identifies important social goals and expectations at work settings for an employee, through interviews with care givers/parents, employers, and the employees. Questions to be included in the ecological inventories are listed in Figure 13. It should be remembered that these social goals and expectations can vary depending on the culture and value system the person comes from. A teacher/employment specialist needs to be sensitive to this culture and value system and to incorporate them into the ecological inventories if possible.

Based on information gathered from the ecological inventories, inputs from co-workers/supervisors, and observations, a teacher or employment specialist can develop a checklist as shown in Figure 14 and have

FIGURE 13
Examples of Questions of Ecological Inventories

1. What is the goal of the person's current employment (e.g., pay, friendship/network, passing time, etc.)?

2. With whom does the person spend the most time at home and at work? What would it take to increase the person's opportunities for relationships with non-disabled co-workers?

3. What is the extent of the person's use of resources at the work setting (e.g., breakroom, gameroom, lunchroom, etc.)?

4. What is the level of personal satisfaction of current employment?

5. What would it take for the person to increase the job satisfaction/quality of worklife?

6. What are the valued roles of the person at the work setting?

7. What would it take to increase the person's role/status at the work setting?

Modified from. "A guide to life-style planning" by O'Brien, In B. Wilcox, & G.T. Bellamy (1987). *A comprehensive guide to the activities catalog: An alternative curriculum for youth and adults with severe disabilities* (pp. 175–189). Baltimore: Paul Brookes Publishing Co.

co-workers/supervisors complete the checklist. In the first column, co-workers/supervisors record "V" if a targeted employee possesses the skills or demonstrates appropriateness in social situations (for items 1 to 5). For items 6 to 10, co-workers/supervisors record "V" if the situations described in the items exist—e.g., the worker spends time with other workers at lunch or break time. In the second column, co-workers/supervisors rate the degree of importance of each statement for the person to be socially accepted at the work setting. After gathering the information on a checklist, a teacher/employment specialist can then compare the "V" with the rating of importance, and can pinpoint the areas for more detailed assessment. For example, if co-workers rated very high on the importance of participating in social functions planned for the employees, but stated that the employee does not participate, then the teacher/employment specialist can focus on this particular social behavior for further assessment.

Assessment of Ecology

Once the initial assessment suggests that there is incongruity between the present level of social acceptance of the person with disabilities and expected social acceptance, then a teacher or employment specialist can proceed to conduct an ecology assessment. The ecology assessment purports to identify whether environment variables might be responsible for the undesirable social acceptance of the person. This assessment

FIGURE 14

An example of an Initial Assessment Tool
for Social Acceptance of an Employee with Disabilities

Worker being evaluated: _____   Date: _____

Evaluator's Status: co-worker _____   Supervisor _____

I. (To be completed by the co-worker or supervisor)

Directions: In the first column, please mark "V" if each statement described for the worker being evaluated is true. In the second column, please indicate the importance of each of the questions when evaluating the social acceptance of the worker whose name appears on the top of this form. Please rate each as:

1. Would not be appropriate in my setting
2. Not important
3. Somewhat important
4. Important
5. Very important

"V"	Rating of importance	
_____	_____	1. The worker is socially competent and skillful)e.g., fits in or gets along with others at the workplace).
_____	_____	2. The worker does not exhibit any behaviors that bother you or others (e.g., gets mad easily).
_____	_____	3. The worker socially interacts with other workers (e.g., approaches others, responds to requests).
_____	_____	4. The appearance and grooming of this worker is appropriate.
_____	_____	5. The worker is a good conversationalist (e.g., taking turns, bringing up topics).
_____	_____	6. The worker spends time with other workers at lunch or break time.
_____	_____	7. The worker is included in social get-togethers among co-workers outside of work.
_____	_____	8. The worker is accepted by other workers in the same job.
_____	_____	9. The worker has a friend(s) at the workplace.
_____	_____	10. The worker is valued by co-workers.

II. (To be completed by teacher/employment specialist) Compare the "V" with the rating of importance for each statement. Circle the statement(s) identified as important by the co-workers/supervisors that the individual does not have. Conduct a further assessment for this(es) circled skills as a next step.

collects data on three variables: physical, social, and organizational ecologies.

Assessment of Physical Ecology: In the physical ecology assessment, the teacher can assess any components of physical settings that might impede social interaction between a person with disabilities and his/her non-disabled co-workers. For example, the teacher can check whether the breakroom/lunchroom has one big rectangular table or several small round tables; or if there is a particular chair (e.g., in a corner) where the person with disabilities prefers to sit, preventing him/her from interacting with others, and so on. Other examples of information include: what is the set-up of a work station? Is the person working alone in the setting or with other co-workers? If the person works with other co-workers, does the physical set-up of furniture impede or facilitate interaction with co-workers when necessary? This information on physical ecology can be easily obtained by observing the person during work, break or lunch.

Assessment of Organizational Ecology: Organizational ecology assessment involves gathering information on policies and program factors that may affect the social interactions and development of support relationship. For example, one can check what shift schedule the person with disabilities has. If the person always works on the weekends when the place is extremely busy, is it even possible for the person to take a break with other co-workers? Is the break schedule of the person with disabilities the same as some other co-workers so that the person can have an opportunity to socially interact with others? Does he/she always take the lunch break with the same group of people? If yes, does it help or impede the person's development of support relationship with co-workers? Does the organizational policy encourage the social integration? The above information can be obtained through interviews with co-workers and through observation of the person during lunch or break.

Assessment of Social Ecology: The social ecology assessment collects information on the non-disabled co-workers' attitude and readiness to develop a support relationship with disabled persons. For example, are the co-workers ready to accept a worker with disabilities as an equal co-worker? Do the other co-workers treat the worker with disabilities fairly with regard to including the person in social activities? Developing a support relationship is different from developing a friendship. A support relationship implies that a person is willing to conduct social activities fairly while friendship implies an emotional relationship that goes beyond offering support and practicing fair play. Evans (1991) points out that the non-disabled person should be given preference regarding with whom he/she wishes to develop a friendship including non-disabled and disabled persons as long as he/she treats the person with disabilities fairly in the course of social activities (e.g., recess). Evans's proposal can be easily transferred into work settings. As long as non-disabled co-workers give equal treatment to employees with disabilities and others during social activities, it can be said that there is a social acceptance/support relationship established. How non-disabled workers behave with a worker with the disabilities during social activities can be noted through observations and/or surveys with co-workers. When using a survey, it is best to use an anonymous survey in order to obtain accurate information. Figure 15 presents sample questions that can be included in the ecology assessment.

FIGURE 15
Sample Questions for Assessment of Ecology

Physical Ecology

1. What is the physical set-up of furniture in a breakroom and/or lunchroom?
2. How does the person utilize the current set-up of furniture in order to interact with other socially (e.g., sitting in a corner not interacting with others)?
3. Does the current physical set-up of furniture impede or enhance social interaction between the person and other co-workers?

Organizational Ecology

1. Does the person take a lunch break with other co-workers?
2. Does the person take a lunch break with the same group of people? If yes, does this help or impede the person's development of support relationship with other co-workers?
3. Does the organizational policy encourage the social interaction of the person with disabilities?

Social Ecology

1. Are the co-workers willing to advocate the person when necessary (e.g., work schedule, break schedule, etc)?
2. Do co-workers make an effort to include the person in social interactions?
3. Do the co-workers treat the person as fairly as they would with other non-disabled co-workers?
4. Do the co-workers view the person positively (e.g., value the person as a co-worker)?

Assessment of Person

Once the ecological assessment is completed, then a teacher employment specialist can proceed to a person-focused assessment. This assessment pinpoints specific skills deficits that may prevent the person from developing a social support relationship with other co-workers. These skills include initiation, expansion, and termination of social interaction, providing positive feedback, acknowledgement, turntaking, etc. Traditional social skills assessment can be included here. One method to assess social skills is to develop a checklist of the important social skills required in initiating social interactions and developing support relationships. The items in the checklist can be generated from literature (e.g., Rusch, 1983) or available instruments (e.g., Meyer, Reichle, McQuater, Vandercook, Evans, Neel, & Kishi, 1985). One comprehensive social skills instrument is the Assessment on Social Competence (Meyer et al., 1985). This instrument measures social competence functions essential for participation in naturally-occurring activities within integrated community environments. The eleven functions measured in the instrument are presented in Figure 16.

A teacher or employment specialist can develop a social skills checklist as shown in Figure 17.

The second method to assess social skills is to observe the person in social situations. One can observe the person for 10 minutes at two times a day whenever social interactions are most likely to occur, e.g., arrival, break, lunch. The observation form as shown in Figure 17 can be used to collect data on initiation, exchange, and duration of social interactions:

1) In the first column, record the date of observation.
2) In the second column, record the times when a conversation begins and ends.
3) In the third column, record the identification of the person who is engaged in social conversation. "T" for the targeted person being assessed or "C" for co-workers. Also the direction of conversation is indicated by an arrow. If possible, verbal statements made between the target person (T) and co-workers (C) are recorded.
4) In the fourth column, record the duration of each statement in measurements of seconds.
5) In the fifth column, record the types of topics: "W" for work-related and "S" for social conversation.
6) When either person begins a new topic, then start a new block of social exchange.
7) Summarize the results in terms of frequency of initiation, exchange, and duration of social interactions, and of the types of topics for each targeted person and for co-workers (See Figure 18).

FIGURE 16
Eleven Social Functions Measured in the Assessment of Social Competence

Social Function	Examples
1. Initiating Interaction	Extending greetings, joining a group
2. Self-regulating	Selecting own chair; selecting a person to talk to, making own choice regarding attending a social party.
3. Following Rules	Playing game by rules, returning to work from break on time, observing lunchroom rules.
4. Providing Positive Feedback	Smiling in response to a person's social actions, giving a compliment, saying social amenities (e.g., "Thank you", "please")
5. Providing Negative Feedback	Saying "No" to reject item or activity, ignoring inappropriate behaviors of co-workers, politely refusing unnecessary help from others.
6. Obtaining Cues	Not insisting an action when a person shows a negative facial expression (e.g., frown)
7. Offering Assistance	Holding door for others, helping pick up an object dropped by a person, relaying information to others.
8. Accepting Assistance	Politely accepting help offered by others (e.g., "Thank you").
9. Indicating Preference	Selecting a choice between two types of social activities (e.g., movie or T.V.), selecting food from a menu.
10. Coping with Negatives	Responding to criticism appropriately, calling another friend if the first friend does not answer.
11. Terminating	Terminating a social interaction appropriately by saying "Bye" or "I have to go," etc., politely terminating a conversation after noticing that the other person is glancing.

Adapted from Meyer, Reichle, McQuarter, Cole, Vandercook, Evans, Neel, and Kishi (1985).

A teacher/employment specialist can use this observation form in order to obtain data on a non-disabled co-worker's social interaction with other non-disabled co-workers (i.e.) initiation, exchange, duration, and topics. Then this data called "normative data" can be compared with the data in the social interaction between the person with disabilities and non-disabled co-workers. The comparison would provide a teacher with an overall picture of the social interaction of the person with disabilities in relation to the non-disabled worker's social interaction.

For more comprehensive information on social participation, a teacher is advised to refer to the Assessment of Social Participation (ASP)

FIGURE 17
A Sample Checklist of Social Skills

Worker _____   Date _____

Directions: Please mark "V" if the worker demonstrates social skill described in each sentence.

_____ Greeting other co-workers at arrival

_____ Sitting or standing at appropriate social distance

_____ Initiating conversations

_____ Exchanging conversations

_____ Staying on topics, changing topics when necessary in a polite manner

_____ Terminating conversations

_____ Giving compliments

_____ Patting back of acquaintance

_____ Looking at speaker when called by name

_____ Smiling when praised or in pleasant social exchange

_____ Accompanying supervisor upon request

_____ Staying near group during social activities

_____ Initiating social/leisure activities with other co-workers

_____ Waiting for turn or activity to begin

_____ Responding appropriately to criticism

_____ Requesting assistance when necessary

_____ Asking other co-workers to stop an annoying behavior

_____ Avoiding unwanted social encounter/attention

_____ Using social amenities (e.g., "Please", "Thank you")

_____ Dressing in an appropriate manner

_____ Sharing things

Adapted from Browder, D. (1991). Assessment of Individuals with Severe Disabilities: An Applied Behavior Approach to Life Skills Assessment. 2nd Edition (pp. 249). Baltimore: Paul Brookes Publishing Co.

developed by Breen et al. (1991). The ASP assesses additional information on turn-taking, participation mode (language or non-language), available opportunities, and acknowledgement.

An important aspect on person-focused assessment is motivation. A person should be motivated to develop social support relationships with

FIGURE 18

A Sample Observation Form for Social Interaction

<u>Social Interaction Observation Form</u>

Worker:_____

Date	Time	People	(Optional)	Duration	Topics
12/10	5:40	C→T	Hi! How are you?	2 Sec	S
	5:50	T→C	Hi!	1 Sec	S
	block 1	T→C	Did you have a nice weekend?	3 Sec	S
		C→T	Oh, yes. I went to my grandma's. It was fun. I've got to see my cousins.	10 Sec	S
		C→T	By the way, are you done with your project?	4 Sec	W
		T→C	Yeah.	1 Sec	W
	block 2	C→T	I am going to the breakroom and get something to drink. You want to come?	9 Sec	S
		T→C	Ok	1 Sec	S
		C→T	Let's go	2 Sec	S

Summary of Social Interaction

		T	C
Initiation			2
Exchange		4	5
Duration		6 Sec	27 Sec
Topic	Social	3	4
	Work	1	1

Definition of Terms

Initiation: a statement that begins a conversation on a new topic.   In this example, only C (co-worker) made two initiations since the co-worker started new topic each time (See C).

Exchange: a statement or question that served to continue a conversation (i.e., led to a verbal response from other person) or appropriately ended a conversational exchange (e.g., "good-bye") in this example, count the number of each T or C that comes before arrow.

Duration: total length of the conversation between the person and interactant. In this example, sum up the length of conversation made by each person.

Topic: count the number of social and work related conversation made by each person.

other co-workers. This motivation may vary from one employee to another. The need for social support relationships can be viewed differently depending on the person's culture and the value system. Their preference/ choices as to the level of social participation should be incorporated in the assessment and intervention. In assessing motivation, a teacher can discuss with the person with disabilities his/her current level of social acceptance at work and the possible consequences that may result from maintaining a low level of social acceptance, e. g., lack of support from co-workers when necessary. And then a teacher can ask if the person is interested in improving social acceptance by modifying his/her own social behaviors.

INTERVENTION

Based on the assessment results, several intervention strategies can be derived. Figure 19 presents the intervention in relation to the assessment. Intervention on ecology introduces a positive social atmosphere and adjusts/modifies positive physical and organizational variables so that a person with disabilities can feel comfortable fitting into social settings at work. As we have seen, a teacher may work out the break schedule for the person with disabilities so that he/she can have an opportunity to interact and develop support relationships with other co-workers. However, it should be remembered that the ecological problems can only be remediated within a possible limit. Modifying the break schedule may not be feasible because there are so few employees that only one person at a time can go on break. In this case, a teacher may intervene to arrange alternative possible social situations for the person, e. g., social get-togethers after work. The feasibility of modification of the environment may be assessed by asking related questions to supervisors. If intervention on environment alone is not enough to improve the level of social acceptance, then a teacher can implement the person-focused intervention programs as a next step. These intervention programs would include social skills training and an intervention to motivate the person. However, when an employee with disabilities already demonstrates inappropriate behaviors, then it would be better to combine ecology and person-focused intervention simultaneously. The following section describes intervention programs and case studies for ecology- and person- focused intervention programs. A social support intervention program designed to build the support network of a person with disabilities is described for the ecology-focused intervention. Both behavioral and cognitive social skills training programs are presented for the person-focused intervention.

Ecology-Focused Intervention: Social Support Intervention

In recent years, increasing attention has been focused on social support interventions in the workplace. As noted earlier, social support interventions are viewed as a way to address the goodness of fit between the individual and the environment by focusing on formal and informal relationships in the work setting. Many professionals in the field maintain that adequate social support in the workplace is a critical factor in employment retention (Hirsch, 1981; Chadsey-Rusch & Rusch, 1988; Karan & Knight, 1986).

FIGURE 19

Intervention Programs for Social Acceptance in Relation to Assessment

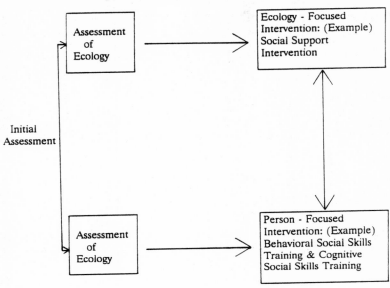

Frequently, this focus on support interventions in the workplace have taken the form of co-worker-implemented job skills training. For example, Likins, Salzberg, Stowitschek, Lignugaris/Kraft and Curl (1989) instructed non-disabled co-workers in procedures for successfully training workers with developmental disabilities in necessary job tasks. Many professionals have argued that using co-workers to facilitate adjustment for workers with disabilities not only enhances social integration (Nisbet & Haggerty, 1988), but it also provides an alternative to use of expensive professional trainers and counselors (Rusch & Menchetti, 1981; Rusch & Minch, 1988).

Siegal (1988) takes an ecosocial systems approach to support intervention. He advocates a "teambuilding" strategy in which key members of the worker's ecosystem agree to provide him or her with the support necessary for meeting agreed-upon goals. These goals may be either task-oriented or social-skill-oriented; in either case, the team works together to better the work situation and adjustment for all the members of the team.

Similarly, the social support intervention advocated by Park, Simon, Tappe, Wozniak, Johnson, and Gaylord-Ross (1991) addresses the ecosocial system of the work place. It is unique in that a co-worker advocate was enlisted to assist the employee with disabilities in fitting into the social culture of the workplace rather than to train specific job tasks or social skills. In this social support intervention, the trainer guided the co-worker advocate, through an eco-social assessment of the workplace, to note how the worker with disabilities fits into that setting. The trainer and co-advocate then established behavior change goals based on this assessment. The advocate was then guided, in the use of a process problem-solving approach, to develop an intervention strategy designed to help the disabled worker fit in socially with co-workers. The trainer and advocate identified and prioritized problems related to helping the worker with disabilities fit into the social culture of the workplace. Then, the two generated alternative solutions and selected an intervention strategy for addressing each problem. Finally, the advocate executed the strategies until the next session with the trainer. The advocate evaluated the effectiveness of each intervention strategy in subsequent sessions with the trainer and the two made modifications as needed.

Chuck: A Case Study

Chuck, a young man with mental retardation, had recently left high school. As a bus boy at a seafood restaurant, Chuck had many opportunities for social contacts with his co-workers. One of his duties was to assist the waitresses and waiters as needed. So good relations would enhance his abilities to do his job well and increase his enjoyment of a job which could become repetitive. His rehabilitation counselor reported that his work production was satisfactory, but that he was shy. He interacted only rarely and in a subdued manner with his co-workers. His counselor believed that he could benefit from a co-worker advocacy program.

As a part of a research project (Park, 1991), Chuck received advocacy help from Beverly, a gregarious waitress who enjoyed working with Chuck at the restaurant. Beverly believed that Chuck could benefit from some encouragement and supportive gestures and agreed to be his advocate for a minimum of six weeks. In weekly 10-minute sessions Beverly met with a member of the project staff and decided on formal and informal activities to do with Chuck. She offered Chuck verbal reminders to greet others, and his initiations noticeably increased during 10-minute observation periods. Beverly reported that his initiations remarkably increased at his arrival time, when he was not observed by the research staff.

Beverly also noticed that Chuck grumbled and complained about work at the end of the day. While his behavior was not unusual for this workplace ecology, Beverly believed that Chuck made negative comments with greater frequency than other co-workers. Beverly decided to counter Chuck's negative comments with positive ones and gave him diversionary tasks to keep him focused on more positive aspects of his work. Beverly reported that while the intervention did not eliminate his negative comments, it did help him to reduce the frequency and bring his behavior more in line with that of other employees.

By the end of the six weeks, Chuck had become comfortable enough with others to joke with them, and had substantially increased the duration of his conversations with others. He and his co-workers appeared more comfortable around each other. During a pre-intervention interview Chuck had stated that he could turn to no one for support at the workplace, but after six weeks of intervention, he believed that Beverly was an important member of his social network at the workplace. He also showed considerable increase on the work setting subscale of a Quality of Work Life Instrument (Seltzer, 1982).

This program had helped Chuck with both his task-related and personal support relationships at the workplace. It had also helped Chuck attain a better social acceptance and experience greater satisfaction with the work setting. By using Beverly as the intervention agent, the research staff was able to be minimally involved in the change process. Beverly, as a resource from the social environment, was able to offer ongoing support and an understanding of the norms for this particular work setting. Also, since the intervention occurred in the natural setting, the proactive situations and consequences were specifically tailored to important behaviors for acceptance at the restaurant.

Person-Focused Intervention: Social Skills Training

In the field of special education social skills training has become an important method for cultivating better social interactions, such as verbal statements, non-verbal gestures, conversations and leisure activities. This training can also improve individual socialization, such as decoding social situations, generating alternatives, and making decisions (Tappe & Gaylord-Ross, in press). Two of the major social skills interventions include behavioral social skills training and cognitive social skills training. This section will explore some ways that these two methods can be applied in the workplace to enhance relationship and acceptance.

Behavioral Social Skills Training. This method of social skills training addresses specific, observable behaviors. The goal of behavioral social skills training is to develop social repertoires so that individuals can attain their goals. This methods often emphasizes such as eye contact, voice tone, and body posture (Trower, 1984). It does not address any cognitive processes which may occur, such as what a person considers when executing a behavior. An instructor or a confederate usually teaches the behaviors through instruction, modeling, role-playing/rehearsal, and feedback for given behaviors.

Specific types of behavioral social skills training can include: peer-mediated training, client-directed training, verbal instruction, task analyzed scripts, rehearsal (role play), corrective feedback, and reinforcement (Tappe & Gaylord-Ross, in press). The methods used are usually based on the best way to solve problem behavioral responses in situations which recur in an individual's daily living. In the workplace someone planning a behavioral intervention would analyze the situation and determine which behaviors are inappropriate and could be changed.

The target behaviors would usually be ones which would be expected to happen often or which could be expected to occur at a given time in the future. The intervention would attempt to increase the individual's social repertoire, so that the individual would then possess the skills to interact more effectively. This method can be used with people at all functioning levels, but is often the only available choice with individuals who have very severe disabilities accompanied by very low cognitive skills.

Tina: A Case Study

Tina, a 23-year old woman, worked in a large department store for 10 hours each week. She has dual sensory impairment with severe mental handicaps. She received aid from the Bay Area Personnel Systems (BAPS) (Gaylord-Ross, Park, Johnson, Lee, & Goetz, in press), a program which assists individuals with multiple sensory and cognitive impairments to function and adjust in the workplace. In this non-sheltered work setting a job coach helped Tina hang clothes on racks, and hand inventory to a co-worker for coding. Tina spent almost all of her time with the job coach and had almost no contact with her non-disabled co-workers. Tina was non-verbal and had no form of gestural communication.

The BAPS program staff designed social routine with response chains to teach Tina. They taught her to orient her face and body toward a co-worker and to extend her hand. During 5 to 10 minute training sessions, project staff encouraged Tina to emit the response chain with co-workers. Actual co-workers were used to encourage social integration and ameliorate the condition of the artificial climate.

During the training a member of the project staff used a time delay procedure for independent practice of the chain. If Tina did not respond in two seconds when an opportunity for greeting someone occurred, a staff member would tap Tina on the chin to orient her face and tap her wrist to encourage her to extend her hand. After two weeks with two-second delays the time was extended to three seconds for one week. In subsequent weeks the intervention became less intrusive and consisted of corrective prompts in which a staff member tapped Tina on the elbow and asked if she would like to say hello. Tina received verbal reinforcement from the staff member, and also the reinforcement for the co-worker who gave an appropriate social response.

Prior to training Tina greeted almost no one and engaged in almost no exchanges. Once social skills training began with a guard at the department store, Tina's exchanges increased to an average of one per session. The training continued with a floor-worker and the number of exchanges increased to include both the greeting and occasional incidental interactions. A third person, another floorworker, participated in training with the result that Tina's exchanges increased. Some sessions included two to five exchanges.

As a by-product of the co-worker training sessions, some of the co-workers became Tina's advocates. They walked her around the store, introduced her to other co-workers, and invited her to join them at break time. Her sensory limitations put her at great risk for social isolation, but social skills training gave Tina the skills to interact with others. In this case the social skills training served a two-fold purpose. It taught Tina how to greet and respond, and it taught individuals within the environment the appropriate manner in which to interact with an individual that they may have been reluctant to approach.

Cognitive Social Skills Training. Cognitive social skills training focuses on assisting the worker with disabilities in understanding social situations and generating his or her own socially skilled behavior. It assumes that cognition, such as inner speech, influences behavior and that by changing cognition, behavior can be modified. Reasoning processes such as interpreting the social environment and determining appropriate behavioral responses are addressed. The individual is instructed in a problem-solving, rule-based process of social behavior (process training) thought to foster skill generalization rather than specific component behaviors (McFall, 1982; Trower, 1984). The effectiveness of this approach has been demonstrated for individuals with mild mental retardation (Park & Gaylord-Ross, 1989) and moderate mental retardation (Collet-Klingenberg, 1990).

Park et al. (1991) employed a process model of social skills training to teach social behavior to workers with disabilities in non-sheltered employment settings. Using an adaptation of McFall's (1982) model, the project staff used training procedures which focused on decoding, decision, performance, and evaluation skills. The project staff taught the reasoning process by training the employees with disabilities in the use of seven corresponding rules: 1) what's happening? 2) what choices? 3) what might happen if . . . ? 4) which is better? 5) how would I do it? 6) do it, and 7) how did I do it? (See Figure 20 and Figure 21).

This cognitive social skill intervention addressed four major components: 1) decoding the social environment; 2) deciding on an appropriate behavioral response; 3) performing the response selected; and 4) evaluating the effectiveness of the response. The first component of the process training, decoding skill, involved the accurate perception and interpretation of one's surroundings to determine "what's happening?" (Rule 1) in a social situation. The second component, decision skill, entailed generating alternative responses to the situation (Rule 2 what choices?), testing each choice (Rule 3—what might happen if . . . ?), and making a selection from the response alternatives (Rule 4—which is better?). The third component, performance, involved determining the appropriate behavioral responses for performing the choice selected (Rule 5—how would I do it?) and the actual performance of the behavior (Rule 6—do it). The last component, evaluation included the evaluation of the effectiveness of the behavior response based on feedback from the social environment (Rule 7—how did I do it?).

In the initial session, the trainer and the worker with disabilities discussed the purpose of social skills training and its importance to social acceptance in the workplace. The seven rules were then presented to the worker with disabilities. To demonstrate the utility of the rules the trainer modeled ways in which the rules could be used in a variety of problem situations. The project staff obtained a commitment from each worker with disabilities to attend training sessions regularly and to study the seven process rules. Together, the trainer and the worker developed a script which applied the seven rules to a problem situation. This script

FIGURE 20
The Seven Rules of the Process Social Skill Training

1. What's Happening?

2. What Choices?   1)
                             OR
                             2)

3. What might happen if—   1) If I _____

    _____

    _____

    _____

    _____

        then _____

    _____

    _____

    _____

    _____

                             2) If I _____

    _____

    _____

    _____

    _____

        then _____

    _____

    _____

    _____

4. Which is Better?

5. How Would I Do It?   I will

6. Do It.

7. How Did I Do it?   If positive,
                              If negative,

included a target behavior for the worker and was used in subsequent social skills training sessions.

Intervention sessions followed a pretest, practice, and post-test format. A variety of methods/tools were used to teach the process rules including flashcards, modeling, and role-play. Memorization of the seven process

FIGURE 21
Example on the Script Based on the Seven Process Rules

Situation: You go to work early and see Victor taking a break. How do you decide what to talk to him about?

1. What's happening?	I'm at work and I want to talk to someone I don't know personally.
2. What Choices?	1) I could talk about something general. OR 2) I could talk about something personal.
3. What Might Happen If—	1) If I talk generally, then Victor may feel comfortable and want to talk to me again. 2) If I talk personally, then Victor may feel uncomfortable and want to avoid me.
4. Which is Better?	Talking generally is better.
5. How Would I Do It?	I would do it by making good eye contact and not playing with my hair or clothing.
6. Do It.	Then I would just do it.
7. How Did I Do It?	After I did it, I would look at Victor's facial expressions. If they were positive, then I'd keep talking to him this way. If they were negative, then I'd change the way I was talking to him.

rules and functional application of social skills were the objectives of the training.

Patty: A Case Study

Patty, a 21 year old disabled woman, worked in the kitchen of a fast food restaurant. Her job was to feed hamburger patties into the automatic broiler, wash utensils, and restock the sandwich preparation area. Her supervisor stated that though Patty had difficulty learning other tasks at the restaurant, she always tried to do what was asked of her and worked hard at the tasks she knew how to perform.

Although Patty was described as a friendly person, she exhibited social behavior which made her co-workers uncomfortable around her. They explained that she often discussed very personal topics with male co-workers whom she did not know well. In addition, while holding a conversation, Patty frequently displayed distracting behavior such as playing extensively with her hair or clothing.

Park, et al. (1991) implemented a 15-week social skills training intervention designed to address Patty's needs. Her target behaviors for the training sessions were appropriate pose and appropriate conversation. Appropriate pose was defined as the use of mannerisms that did not distract from the conversation at hand. Appropriate conversation was defined as responses that best met the demands of the social situation given the time, the location, and the relationship with a conversational partner. Patty's social skill training script focused primarily on appropriate conversation. Appropriate pose was addressed in the performance component (Rule 5—how would I do it?) of the training program (refer to Figure 21).

The trainer met with Patty one time weekly for fifteen weeks. The sessions took place in the dining room of the fast food restaurant at mid-morning when there were not many customers around. Patty was very distractable throughout the training sessions. Consequently, it was the fifth training session before she showed any retention of the process rules. However, from that point on she made slow but steady progress in memorizing and applying the rules. By the end of training, Patty had mastered approximately 86% of the process steps.

Conversational skills ratings completed by Patty's co-workers and the project staff indicated increased appropriate conversation and pose at the conclusion of the social skills sessions. One male co-worker reported that Patty fit in better with others on the job; that she was like "part of the crowd." The follow-up assessment completed six weeks after the intervention revealed an overall maintenance of the increases gained through the intervention.

Social Support and Social Skills Training in Combination

It is clear that both social support intervention and social skills training provide useful means for promoting social acceptance in work settings. Though they focus on different aspects of the social context, their intervention roles are complimentary. As some of the previous case studies point out, social support interventions often influence a person's social skills, and in a similar manner social skills training can effect the amount of social support that a person perceives as available. In Chuck's case his advocate spontaneously chose to encourage Chuck to initiate more greetings of his fellow co-workers, and offered him instruction and reinforcement. In Tina's case the project staff enlisted co-workers to help train Tina, which gave the co-workers a better understanding of appropriate interactions for incorporating Tina into the social environment.

In facilitating a person-environment fit, (or maximizing the social ecological balance), an intervention should address both the individual's skill level and also the environment in which behaviors will occur. An individual should possess the ability to socially function at a level appropriate to the person's abilities. Likewise, an environment should be receptive, to that particular individual's behaviors. The environment should also offer opportunities for social interaction to occur, and have some reinforcing qualities to help assure that appropriate behaviors will recur.

If social skills training and social support interventions are to occur in a single individual's case, it is often more expedient to offer the social skills training first if an individual does not possess appropriate skills to interact with others (Park et al., 1991). Individuals with inappropriate social behavior will not be reinforcing to advocates or other supporters who offer them aid. The inappropriate behavior may discourage a supporter from offering further support. However, if an individual does possess social skills but does not practice (e. g., a shy person), then social support intervention may be offered first so that a more positive social climate can be provided. The social support intervation (modification of ecology) may result in more time efficiency and cost effectiveness than the social skills training.

Implementing the Interventions

The desired goal in implementing either social support or social skills interventions is to achieve social adjustment in the workplace by maximizing the ecological match between the individual with disabilities and the social environment. Initially, when a placement is made, the job developer should make every effort to find an environment which will be receptive to the person, accepting of both disabilities and capabilities. An ideal match will rarely occur spontaneously, and often adaptations will need to be made to facilitate the acceptance of the individual with disabilities. Often the workplace will be most receptive to minimalist interventions. Interventions which are not disruptive to the productivity goals of the workplace and which do not require excessive time commitments will probably be best received.

The case studies discussed above involved minimal time commitments from the co-worker participants: either 10 minute per week meetings with a job trainer, with time commitments on the job interspersed over the day's work, or participation in training periods which lasted less than five minutes. Specific skill training or cognitive plan developments with a person with disabilities can occur initially with a job trainer during work, breaks or outside of the job, with follow up in short time increments in the actual job setting.

In considering the fit of an individual with the environment, job developers and trainers need to consider the reciprocal influences and interdependencies which occur in an ecological system (Karan & Knight, 1986). Both the workers at the site and the individual with disabilities should bring something to the relationship in order to ensure success. Several qualities of co-workers advocates which could contribute to successful interactions would include: an ability to communicate with the employee with disabilities, knowledge and acceptance of the social norms in the workplace, social acceptance by their fellow workers, longevity at the work site, and an understanding of the employee's disabilities and capabilities.

The employee with disabilities may not be able to achieve one-to-one reciprocity (Gaylord-Ross, et al., in press), but should be able to make at least some contribution to the relationship. Qualities of employee with disabilities which could facilitate a contribution would include: an ability to respond in some way to social overtures, a desire to fit into the social norms of the workplace, and a willingness to learn acceptable and appropriate behaviors for the given site.

Job developers cannot always make placements based on an ideal match. For example, sometimes job developers must make a decision to place someone at an available position where workers tend to be transient, and social norms are nebulous. When this happens the vocational placement agency should take responsibility to adapt a situation and promote better relations to the greatest extent possible.

REFERENCES

Breen, C. G., Kennedy, C. H. & Haring, T. G. (1991). *Social Context Research Project: Methods for Facilitating the Inclusion of Students with Disabilities in Integrated School and Community Centers.* University of California, Santa Barbara.

Brickey, M. P., Browning, L. J. & Campbell, K. M. (1982). Vocational histories of sheltered workshop employees placed in projects with industry and competitive job. *Mental Retardation, 20,* 52–57.

Bronfrenbenner, U. (1979). *The Ecology of Human Development.* Cambridge, MA: Harvard University Press.

Chadsey-Rusch, J. & Rusch, R. R. (1988). The ecology of the workplace. In R.

Gaylord-Ross (Ed.), *Vocational Education for Persons with Special Needs* (pp. 234–255). Palo Alto, CA: Mayfield.

Chadsey-Rusch, J. (1986). Identifying and teaching valued social behaviors. In F. Rusch (Ed.), *Competitive Employment Issues and Strategies* (pp. 273–288). Baltimore: Paul Brookes.

Collect-Klingenberg, L., & Chadsey-Rusch, J. (1991). Using a cognitive-process approach to teach social skills. *Education and Training in Mental Retardation, 26*(3), 258–270.

Evans (1991). *Fair Work, fair play: Patterns of interaction and social cognition in elementary classrooms mainstreaming students with severe handicaps.* Presented at the Robert Gaylord-Ross Memorial Symposium on the Status of Social Skills Training in Special Education and Rehabilitation: Present and Future Trends. Nashville: Vandabilt University.

French, J., Caplan, R. & Van Harrison, R. (1982). The Mechanisms of Job Stress and Strain. New York: Wiley.

Gaylord-Ross, R., Park, H. S., Johnson, S., Lee, M. & Goetz, L. (In press). Social communication and co-worker training for deaf-blind supported employees. *Behavior Modification.*

Greenspan, S., & Shoultz, B (1981). Why mentally retarded adults lose their jobs: Social competence as a factor work adjustment. *Applied Research in Mental Retardation, 2,* 23–38.

Hirsh, B. J. (1981). Social networks and the coping process. In B. H. Gottlieb (Ed.), *Social Networks and Social Support.* Beverly Hills: Sage.

House, J. (1981). *Work Stress and Social Support.* Reading, MA: Addison Wesley.

Karan, O. C. & Knight, C. B. (1986). Developing support networks for individuals who fail to achieve competitive employment. In F. R. Rusch (Ed.), *Competitive Employment Issues and Strategies,* (pp. 241–255). Baltimore: Paul Brookes.

Likins, M., Salzberg, C., Stowitschek, J., Lignugaris/Kraft, B. & Curl, R. (1989). Co-worker implemented job training: The use of coincidental training and quality-control checking on the food preparation skills of trainees with mental retardation. *Journal of Applied Behavior Analysis, 22* (4), 381–393.

McFall, R. (1982). A review and reformulation of the concept of social skills. *Behavioral Assessment, 4,* 1–33.

Meyer, L., Reichle, J., McQuarter, R., Cole, D., Vandercrook, T., Evans, I., Neel, R. & Kishi, G. (1985). *Assessment of Social Competence.* (ASC): A scale of social competence functions. Minneapolis: University of Minnesota Consortium Institute for the Education of Severely Handicapped Learners.

Nisbet, J., & Hagner, D. (1988). Natural supports in the workplace: A reexamination of support employment. *Journal of the Association for the Severely Handicapped, 13* (4), 260–267.

Park, H–S. & Gaylord-Ross, R. (1989). A problem solving approach to social skills training in employment settings with mentally retarded youth. *Journal of Applied Behavior Analysis, 22*(4), 373–380.

Park, H–S., Simon, M., Tappe, P., Wozniak, T., Johnson, B. & Gaylord-Ross, R. (1991). Effects of co-worker advocacy program and social skills training on the social interaction of employees with mild disabilities. *Journal of Vocational Rehabilitation,* 1(4), 73–90.

Rogers-Warren, A., & Warren, S. F. (1977). The developing ecobehavioral psychology. In A. Rogers-Warren & S. F. Warren (Eds.), *Ecological Perspectives in Behavior Analysis* (pp. 3–8). Baltimore: University Park Press.

Rusch, F. (1983). Competitive employment. In M. E. Snell (Ed.), *Systematic Instruction of Moderately and Severely Handicapped.* Columbus, OH: Charles. E. Merrill.

Rusch, F., & Menchetti, B. (1981). Increasing compliant work behaviors in a nonsheltered work setting. *Mental Retardation, 19,* 107–111.

Rusch, F. & Minch, K. (1988). Identification of co-worker involvement in supported employment: A review and analysis. *Research in developmental Disabilities, 9,* 247–254.

Salzberg, C. L., Lignugaris/Kraft, B. & McCuller, G. L. (1988). Reasons for job loss: A review of employment termination studies of mentally retarded workers. *Research in Developmental Disabilities, 9,* 153–170.

Siegel, S. (1988). The career ladder program: Implementing re-ed principles in vocational settings. *Behavioral Disorders, 14* (1), 16–26.

Siegel, S., Park, H-S., Gumpel, T., Ford, J., Tappe, P. & Gaylord-Ross, R. (1990). Research in special education. In R. Gaylord-Ross (Ed.), *Issues and Research in Special Education: Vol. 1* (pp. 173–242). New York: Teacher's College Press.

Tappe, P. & Gaylord-Ross, R. (in press). Social support and transitional coping. In R. Gaylord-Ross (Ed.), *Issues and Research in Special Education: Vol. 2.* New York: Teacher's College Press.

Trower, P. (1984). A radical critique and reformulation: From organism to agent. In P. Trower (Ed.), *Radical approaches to social skills training* (pp. 47–88). New York: Croom Helm.

Willems, E. P. (1977). Steps toward an ecobehavioral technology. In A. Rogers-Warren & S. F. Warren (Eds.), *Ecological Perspective in Behavior Analysis* (pp. 39–61). Baltimore: University Park Press.

Chapter Seven

BILINGUAL METHODS

This chapter will explain some history leading toward the establishment of bilingual methods. The chapter will also help define some of the different methods that are used in teaching students who are culturally and linguistically different. Additionally, this chapter will explain how bilingual methods can be used to teach the linguistically different who are more severely disabled or are autistic.

HISTORY OF BILINGUALISM OR DUAL LANGUAGE INSTRUCTION

Bilingualism has been common since ancient times. It is not unusual to read in history books where groups of people who conquered various lands would soon require the people of these lands to begin speaking the dominant language of these people. In the sixth century B.C.E., for instance, ancient Greeks penetrated and dominated large areas of the Mediterranean. These particular groups of people who conquered lands in the sixth century spoke Greek and had no interest in replacing the local language with their own Greek language. Still, many of the conquered people started to function in languages other than their own native language (Lessow-Hurley, 1990).

In the ancient world, knowing more than one language was the norm. In ancient times, the need to know more than one language was tied to literacy (Lessow-Hurley, 1990). Also, dual language instruction was generally the norm because materials were written in various languages, and if the person knew only one language, these people would not be able to read important material because it was written in one of several languages.

In Europe, bilingualism has always been valued. The Romans, for instance, had the students enrolled in their classes learn Latin regardless of which language the students knew first. The importance of knowing Latin has continued until fairly recently or until the rise of nationalism and the Protestant Reformation caused the use of vernaculars for writing and education.

The Jewish people, for example, used Hebrew for worship. Even though Jewish people have been located in different places, they have still used Hebrew to worship. It is important to note that the Jewish people also knew and some still do know and use the Yiddish language, which is related to German and has, in some ways, entered our English language, for example, the words bagel and glitch which come to us from Yiddish.

In our present day, bilingualism is seen in almost every part of the world (Lessow-Hurley, 1990). Japan and the area once known as West Germany can be labeled as monolingual countries, and even these two countries have many people who speak languages other than the first languages of those nations.

The following countries are officially bilingual or multilingual: Canada, Belgium, Finland, Cyprus, Israel, Ireland, and Czechoslovakia (Lessow-Hurley, 1990). It should be noted that just because the countries are labeled bilingual, not all of the people living in these bilingual countries are bilingual or know more than one language. Often only a small percentage of the country use both languages frequently. Official bilingualism means simply that more than one language may be used in transactions with the government or in the schools. Different countries have and adopt various policies with the languages they endorse.

Some countries, like India, for instance, have more languages than their governmental policies recognize. Hindi is the official language of India and is the most widely used. Additionally, in India, English is spoken plus fourteen other languages, and all of these are officially recognized in the constitution.

In China and the Soviet Union, many different languages are spoken and represented in their large territories.

In Paraguay, for example, Guaraní (an indigenous Indian language) is the national language and is the official first language of ninety percent of Paraguay's people. Although, Spanish is the official language of Paraguay and is the official language used in the schools and for other government business. In Paraguay, over half of the population are bilingual, but Guaraní is a cherished language and is the language of choice for personal intimacy and for poetry (Lassow-Hurley, 1990).

In the United States, when the U.S. Constitution was written, the founding fathers made a decision not to establish an official national language. Recently, local efforts have resulted in policies that proclaim the official language to be English. Regardless of these policies, the United States is a multilingual nation with native American languages, Spanish, and other diverse languages of its immigrants who have contributed to making the United States a linguistically diverse nation. It should be noted here that when some people or groups characterize themselves as resisting the instruction of more than one language in the schools or becoming resistant to cultural and linguistic diversity, that is considered language parochialism. Language parochialism might be described as an attitude about language that holds multilingualism in low regard and fails to acknowledge the benefits of language sophistication (Lessow-Hurley, 1990). Language parochialism will be described later in this chapter.

By contrast to some local areas of the United States where efforts are made to proclaim English as the only language of instruction, in countries like Sweden, China, and Canada dual language instruction is supported by the government through education. People are often surprised to further discover that dual language instruction has been widely available in the United States since the beginning of its history as a nation, for the most part because of the immigration that has been constant in United States history.

In the nineteenth century, non-English or dual language instruction was offered in more than a dozen states. Some of the languages where dual language instruction was evident include German, Swedish, Norwegian, Danish, Polish, Italian, Czech, French, and Spanish (Ovando & Collier, 1985). Immigrants and Native Americans also made instruction in two languages available for their children, attempting to keep culture loss from occurring.

Native Americans, for example the Cherokee, used bilingual materials in such ways that they increased English literacy among their people to a higher level than that of the white populations of either Texas or Arkansas (Castellanos, 1983).

The Native American tribes of the Southwest were very successful in dealing with Europeans. Some of the tribes were able to develop writing systems. This ability helped to facilitate dual language instruction. The government has allowed the dual language instruction among the Native Americans, particularly tribes of the Southwest, due to political expediency. Those Indian school systems that were permitted to exist survived the

Civil War but unfortunately were later destroyed in the latter part of the nineteenth century (Weinberg, 1977).

Additionally to Native Americans maintaining their native languages, immigrant Germans fared well in maintaining their language through dual language instruction during the nineteenth century. Many German immigrants were heavily concentrated in the Midwest and were in some ways isolated and were not considered a threat even though they controlled and financed their local schools and thus exerted political strength also on the communities.

In 1840, German-English dual language programs were instituted in Ohio, and, by the turn of the century, 17,584 students were studying German in dual language programs in primary grades primarily (Lessow-Hurley, 1990). Dual language programs were also widespread in Missouri (Jyack, 1974). In 1880 German was taught in 52 of the 57 public schools in St. Louis, and German-English programs attracted not only German children, but also Anglo-American children who learned German as a second language (Escamilla, 1980).

By the end of the nineteenth century, Irish Catholics moved into the Midwest, and some bias was provoked by the influx of Irish immigrants. Additionally, with the immigration of the Irish immigrants a wave of anti dual language instruction was evident. Thus, the Irish and German suffered anti foreign feelings that were much in evidence in the second half of the eighteenth century.

With the coming of World War I, anti-German feeling was brought to a head and legislation aimed at eliminating German language instruction caused the collapse of dual language programs around the country. At the turn of the century, only fourteen of the forty-five states mandated English as the sole language of instruction in the schools. By 1923, a total of thirty-four of the forty-eight states had English-only instructional policies (Castellanos, 1983).

Two occurrences of World War I were isolationism and nationalism, and these added to the anti-sentiment toward dual language instruction. Instruction in foreign languages in public schools was virtually eliminated in the period between the first and second World Wars. In the 1950's interest was reawakened in dual language instruction. Then Sputnik was launched by the Soviet Union. This event inspired the passage of the National Defense Education Act (1958). It was now considered important to have knowledge of foreign languages for the national defense of our country.

Further, the Cuban revolution (1958) brought a flood of educated Cuban refugees to Florida. In 1963, Coral Way Elementary School was established, in order to offer dual language instruction for Cuban and non-Hispanic children. The program was designed for dual language instruction and was not compensatory nor remedial.

With all of this activity taking place, the nation was in the midst of political activity favoring expanding civil rights. Additionally there seemed to be a powerful affirmation made for bilingual programs. Bilingual programs were established in Texas, California, New Mexico, New Jersey, and Arizona (Amhert & Meléndez, 1985).

In 1965 the Elementary and Secondary Education Act (ESEA) was approved by Congress. The main purpose of the Act was to equalize educational opportunities. The Bilingual Education Act, or Title VII, of the ESEA was signed into law in 1968. While Title VII did not mandate bilingual education, it provided funds for districts to establish programs that used primary language instruction to assist limited English proficient children. In amendments which followed, Title VII funds were allocated for teacher training, research, information dissemination, and program support.

Also in 1974, in the care of Lawrence Nichols, it was held, on the basis of Title VII of the Civil Rights Act (1964), that children must receive equal access to education regardless of their inability to speak English.

In 1971, Massachusetts was the first state to mandate bilingual education. By 1983, bilingual education was permitted in all 50 states, and 9 states had laws requiring some form of dual language instruction for students with limited English proficiency (Ovando & Collier, 1985).

In the 1980s lack of government support for primary language instruction, coupled with having many immigrants come to the United States, weakened support for dual language instruction in many areas. California, with a population of over 600,000 limited English proficient children, allowed its bilingual education to lapse in June 1987.

The many immigrants that have continued to come to the United States have inevitably caused a large demand for teachers who are able to teach dual language learners.

BILINGUAL METHODS

In this section methods which can be effectively used with limited English proficient students will be discussed. Also, bilingual methods which can be used with moderate-to-severely disabled and autistic students will be presented. Further, the term *bilingualism* and *linguistic minority student* will be defined.

Bilingualism is defined as the person's ability to process two languages (Williams and Snipper, 1990). The term *language* encompasses listening, speaking, reading, and writing. *Proficiency* means the ability of a person to process language in listening, speaking, reading, and writing. Bilingual proficiency would involve the following (Williams & Snipper, 1990):

1) It would involve understanding the message in each of the languages spoken.
2) It would involve being able to respond to each of the languages in manner that is appropriate to the situation.
3) It would involve being able to respond to each of the languages in a manner that is appropriate to the situation.

Each skill noted above may be performed with various levels of competence.

The term *linguistic minority student* refers to a student who is a native speaker of a language other than English; within this category there is a wide diversity. The term may refer to those students of varying degrees of literacy who have just migrated with their families to the United States; to students who are living in the United States and learning both languages simultaneously; to second generation students who prefer to speak English at schools and their native languages at home; and finally, to migrant children who may be represented in any of the above descriptions (Nuttall, Landrum and Goldman, 1984).

With the growing numbers of minority students in special as well as regular education, there is a need for teachers to better understand how second language learners learn. According to Yates (1988) the numbers of Black, Latino, and Asian citizens are dramatically increasing, with Latinos representing the fastest growing population in this country (*Austin American Statesman*, 1986). The Census Bureau reported that as of March 1985, the Latino population in the United States had increased some 16% in a little over 5 years, compared to the national population increase of 3.3%. Latinos now represent 16.9 million people in the United States, an increase of approximately 2.3 million since the 1980 census. Reich (1986) projects that by the year 2080, the Latino population in the United States, now representing 7% of the population, will have increased to 19%. Currently there are approximately 247 Black mayors in the

United States, and almost 6,000 Black elected officials. In 1986, there were 3,202 elected Latino officials (Lim, 1986).

The political power and influence of minorities is undeniable in a nation which, by the year 2000, will have 260 million people, one of every three of whom will be either Black, Latino, or Asian-American. A dramatic and clearly defined increase in the number of language minorities has occurred in this country (Omark and Erickson, 1983). In 1980, there were 14 or 15 major language groups with almost 2,400,000 students between the ages of 5 and 14; this number of language minority students is projected to increase by approximately one third by the year 2000. By far, the largest minority group is Spanish-speaking, with more than two-thirds of the entire language minority population being represented by Spanish speakers. The number of Spanish speakers in this country is projected to increase some 48% between 1980 and the year 2000, numbering more than 22 million persons by the year 2000 (Macías, 1985).

Thus with such overwhelming statistics, it becomes obvious that it is extremely important to continue efforts to prepare teachers who are currently teaching and will be teaching language minority students in years to come. In reviewing material for this chapter, this writer came across very few specific and/or detailed articles or information on bilingual or dual language instruction methods. It became apparent to this writer that more close ties need to be developed by bilingual and special educators. In order for the future teacher to develop appropriate methods in dealing with language teaching an overview of the history of language teaching efforts together with their successes and failures, seems useful. In the section which follows, this writer will explain some of the dual language instruction methods which can be useful to teachers, parents, and care providers who teach second language learners.

Following this section the writer will explain how she has used many of the dual language instruction methods with minority students who are culturally and linguistically different.

GRAMMAR-TRANSLATION

This method emerged fully to be used in the 19th century. William Lily, assisted by, Erasmus, wrote the first English grammar in modern English. During the Renaissance simple English paragraphs describing every day situations were carefully analyzed in the classroom and then translated into Latin. What was done in the Grammar-Translation Method was to examine each word or phrase, explain its grammatical use and then equivalents were identified in the mother tongue. In the Grammar-Translation Method, there is a focus on learning rules and working with written texts. It is a remnant of the study of Latin grammar which was highly valued in the Middle Ages (Lessow-Hurley, 1990). During this time, Latin texts were increasingly translated into vernaculars. There was a resistance to formal study of modern languages, a resistance which continued well into the 18th century. Francois Gouin, a 19th century Latin teacher from France, invented or developed this method, which originally involved learning a new language through an ordered series of concepts that systematically introduce new vocabulary and grammatical patterns (Lessow-Hurley, 1990).

A key transition figure was John Valentín Meidinger who helped to formalize the new methodology of the Grammar-Translation Method. In the changes Meidinger made, grammatical rules and paradigms were provided as the basis for translating native-language sentences into the foreign language (Bowen, Madsen & Hilferty, 1980).

James Hamilton (1764–1829) also made some contributions to the Grammar Translation Method. He argued that language instruction should be inductive. He noted that the student's initial exposure must be to reading in the target language, but text he wrote was found to be too difficult for most of his students to understand.

Other texts were developed which utilized the Grammar-Translation Method. (The chief weakness of many of these texts were that they were contrived and had many unnatural sentences.) These unnatural sentences were unlikely to promote genuine language competence. Some examples found in these books were items such as these: "The cat of my aunt is more treacherous than the dog of your uncle." "My sons have brought the mirrors of the duke." (Bowen, Madsen, & Hilferty, 1985).

Another Grammar-Translation advocate was Karl Plotz (1819–1881). He utilized the two-part rule/translation format; his texts attempted to use the vernacular to master the foreign language. In what Plotz contributed to the method a person memorized words, translated sentences, and drilled on irregular verbs. Later there was more emphasis on memorizing, as well as repeating and applying grammatical rules with their exceptions. That remained the main focus—repeating and applying grammatical rules with their exceptions. Later, reading was added, and students had to write full compositions in the foreign language they were studying or learning.

As more textbooks became available and there was an increase in the enrollment in language classes, the acceptance of the Grammar-Translation Method was increased. The Grammar-Translation Method was an easy method for the teacher to use. Classes could be taught in the students' native language, with little teaching skill or foreign-language speaking skill needed by the instructor. The objectives were limited, and teachers felt the objectives were also attainable. What made this method especially popular with the teachers were vocabulary lists, printed grammar rules, and sample sentences to translate, followed by reading selections. Further, the directness or ease of translation and the utilization of the students' native-language proficiency were also appealing features. Also what made teachers enjoy this method was that the study of language could be entwined with some of the most beautiful and profound literature of the ages. With this approach, plastic and void-like contexts were avoided.

Some of the disadvantages of this approach or method were the inefficiency of instruction, and limited results in terms of communication. The most widely seen limitation of communication using this method was that there was a lack of oral proficiency or naturalness of speaking abilities which must be developed if a person truly is learning to speak the language.

THE NATURAL METHOD

The Natural Method (1890) followed the Grammar-Translation Method. It seemed almost like a reaction against translation and grammar study. There was reluctance to use books in the classroom, and textbooks were used only for induction insights. In this approach the child was to be immersed in the language, and the student was to formulate his/her own generalizations. There were monologues by the teacher. There were questions made by the teacher, and the student responded. All of this was to be done in the foreign language being studied. There was much pantomime which accompanied the talking. There was attentive listening and some repetition. The student started to associate certain acts and objects with certain combinations of sounds. The student eventually started to reproduce foreign words and phrases. Vocabulary rapidly extended. The student was not encouraged to use his/her mother tongue, so the student could be forced to begin using the foreign language with greater facility and ease. Later, the student was allowed to see the foreign language in print. Much later, grammar was introduced and with the introduction of grammar came learning to write phrases which were orally dictated to the student. This approach emphasized games, activities and demonstrations. All of this was encouraged to enhance motivation and understanding of the foreign language (Bowen, Madsen & Hilferty, 1985).

Some of the forerunners of the Natural Method include Lemare, Dufief, and Payne, who emphasized self-reliance among the students. They also encouraged the students to learn much of the material by induction rather than memorization. Lemare recommended that rules not be given to students. Later there was much emphasis given on having students read and engage in conversation. It was stressed that teachers should be inventive so that influences from the environment (sneezes, wagon noises, flower scents, lighting, etc.) could be incorporated in the lesson.

Francois Gouin, writing about this method in 1880, provided another technique that could be added to this approach. He advocated that students should actively engage in doing what they spoke about, first in their native language, then in the target language. Thus, if a child had visited a "mill," for instance, the child was encouraged to speak and actively do all she/he spoke about, first in the native language, then in the target language (Bowen, Madsen and Hilferty, 1985).

Some of the criticisms which followed about this approach were that there was a lack of a system, and there was a heavy demand on teachers to create their own teaching procedures (Bowen, Madsen and Hilferty, 1985). By the end of the 19th century, the Natural Method was no longer recommended as a means of teaching another or foreign language to students, because using this method was motivational. In this century, we see great value in this method because it fosters teaching of natural, contextualized language in everyday situations. It is also highly valued today because its approach incorporates both verbal and non-verbal activity to learn the foreign language.

It should be noted that suitable textbooks and teacher guidelines are lacking in this method. Still, the motivational value of the approach makes this technique highly desirable for teachers who want to motivate students to learn a foreign language (Bowen, Madsen, Hilferty, 1985).

THE PHONETIC METHOD

This method appeared in the 19th century. It resembles the "natural" and the "psychological" schools in that it takes the modern spoken language as a basis and at first relies mainly on oral instruction, using as far as possible the foreign language itself as a medium of communication (Bowen, Madsen, & Hilferty, 1985). It is systematically constructed. It begins with a training of the ear and the vocal organs, the pupils being thoroughly drilled in the vowels and consonants of the strange tongue, printed texts are used, but only in phonetic notation. Objects, pictures, and maps are constantly displayed, and every effort is made to familiarize the class with the surroundings, the institutions, the habits, the character, and the mode of thought of the people whose language they are learning (Bowen, Madsen, Hilferty, 1985). Inflections and syntax are studied inductively. Composition consists first of the oral and written reproduction of matter already heard or read, then of combinations of familiar phrases. Systematic grammar is reserved for a later stage, and translation comes last of all. In 1902, the Phonetic Method became the official language teaching method in both France and Germany (Bowen, Madsen and Hilferty).

THE DIRECT METHOD

In this method teachers rejected translation as the cornerstone of language instruction. They tended to favor a period of listening prior to teaching students how to speak, and quite generally the teaching of receptive skills prior to productive skills. (Bowen, Madsen and Hilferty).

Speech, not writing, was viewed as the basis of language. Pronunciation —not phonetics—was to be taught in class; the phonograph was commonly utilized. (An oral-aural approach was used at beginning levels with oral readings introduced later on.) In the oral-aural approach, the teacher gave information which the students listened to and later repeated it orally. Books could be used with caution later on, though some teachers disapproved, fearing that either the printed word might weaken pronunciation skills, or simply because texts were so prominent in Grammar-Translation classes, which they found faulty. In this method they began to advocate graded sequencing of materials from easy to difficult, and they agreed that language was a skill or habit. In this method, it was favored that modification of teaching approaches should be made according to the age or background of students. (Bowen, Madsen and Hilferty, 1895).

Some of the criticisms of this method include lack of teacher training and materials, the relatively unstructured coursework, unrealistic requirements for lesson preparation, exacting requirements for teacher expertise in the foreign language, exhausting drains on teacher energy during lesson presentations—all caused frustration and exhaustion among students who were being taught by this approach (Bowen, Madsen and Hilferty, 1985).

OTHER METHODS USED WITH SECOND LANGUAGE LEARNERS

Immersion Programs

Immersion programs provide dual instruction in language one and language two over a period of years until students are proficient in both languages (Williams & Snipper, 1990). The goal of immersion may be either bilingualism or monolingualism, as will be shown.

In the United States, there have been two types of immersion programs. One is directed toward mainstream English-speaking students and has bilingualism as its goal. Language-minority students in an immersion program receive content-area instruction in English. This type of immersion is called *submersion* because of the social difficulties associated with being a minority student in a language-majority classroom (Williams and Snipper, 1990).

The main goal of immersion is improved academic performance in English. The goal is to give students the general language skills and the specific academic literacy skills they need to compete with Native English-speaking children. According to Williams & Snipper (1990) the goal of giving the students general language skills and the specific academic literacy skills they need to learn English is rarely realized because it is linked to the broader goal of English monolingualism. This broader goal fails to recognize the importance of native-language skills in developing second-language proficiency among students. In attempting to do away with the native language, language-minority immersion programs destroy the very foundation of students' eventual performance in English.

Several studies have examined the academic performance of children in immersion programs, and they reveal majority-language children fare better than minority-language children (California State Department of Education, 1984; Phillipson & Skutnabb-Kangas, 1986). (Both the St. Lambert Experiment in Canada and the Culver City Immersion Project in California have shown positive results in native- and second-language academic achievement with mainstream, English-speaking children who were immersed in French in the first case and Spanish in the second.) Other studies reveal that immersion programs in German, Spanish, and French for mainstream native). English speakers in the United States report similar results (Samuels & Griffore, 1979).

Lambert (1983) notes that the above findings are consistent with his view that immersion for majority students constitutes additive bilingualism. He maintains that these students can surpass the achievement of non-participating peers in their native language, while enjoying the benefits of the enrichment provided by the second language. Lambert (1983) further adds that immersion for language-minority students constitutes subtractive bilingualism, because the programs are not specifically designed for them and are, in fact, harmful to children's identities and their social development. Cummins (1980) suggests that prestige, a positive self-concept, and society's support for the dominant language facilitate the success of language immersion or immersion for students learning a second language for the majority language children.

Some different results concerning immersion programs than the results of Lambert and Cummins have been reached by Modiano (1968). Modiano, working in Chiapas, Mexico, found that immersion reduced students' academic achievement levels. This was also noted by Skutnabb-Kangas (1984). Also, MacNamara (1966) after evaluating immersion education in Ireland, reported negative effects on the cognitive development of bilingual students. MacNamara (1966) concludes that a bilingual pays for his L_2 skills by a decrease in L_1 skills.

It should be noted that language is not the only principal factor affecting academic performance. A large body of research indicates that such factors as family and teacher expectations significantly affect student achievement (Graves, 1981; Gundlach, 1981, 1982; Harste, Burke & Woodward, 1983; Heath, 1983). Perl and Wilson (1986) conclude also that after studying student writers for four years, the major factor governing classroom writing performance is teacher expectations.

Studies above note that teachers themselves may contribute to low academic achievement among language-minority students. Teachers often expect second-language learners to have more problems with reading and writing than their mainstream counterparts. Teachers further define language-minority students as low achievers among other teachers, administrators, mainstream peers, and society. Many of these low expectations become a self-fulfilling prophecy for the language-minority students.

Concurrent Translation

This method is not well understood but is commonly used. This method involves using two languages interchangeably during instruction. Some of the criticisms of this approach include the following:

1) Teachers often code-switch, assuming that they are engaged in concurrent translation. Code switching is linguistically coherent but often the switches a bilingual speaker may make in ordinary conversation do not necessarily meet instructional objectives for language development or delivery of content.
2) Also, concurrent translation often approximates direct translation; students quickly learn to tune out the language they do not understand, waiting for the information they do.
3) Concurrent translation can be tiring for a teacher to implement. Two teachers, or a teacher and an aide, can implement the method, assuming there is available and sufficient staffing.
4) Teachers often overestimate the amount of time they spend using the children's primary language and, in fact, spend a disproportionate amount of time speaking English.

The new Concurrent Approach, which was developed by Rodolfo Jacobson (1987), suggests using a structured form of code-switching for delivery of content instruction. Jacobson carefully plans the code-switching which is to be done (Lessow-Hurley, 1990). In the carefully planned switching, all of the language switches are made at the completion of a thought group. Jacobson notes that planned switches are justifiable for several purposes:

1) Conceptual reinforcement and review, to assure that all children have mastered the lesson material.
2) Lexical enrichment to give children the vocabulary necessary to discuss a particular subject in both languages.
3) Appropriateness for curriculum—this may mean that ethnically related events or subjects may be treated in the appropriate language.

Preview—Review

This approach incorporates elements of the new Concurrent Approach. In preview-review, content areas are previewed in one language, presented in another, and reviewed in the first. This method may be especially useful in the upper primary and secondary levels, where content materials like science or social studies textbooks may not be readily available in minority languages.

Cooperative Learning

This method departs from the traditional whole-class instructional format and allows for first and second language development. In cooperative learning, the class is divided into teams. The members of the teams work together and rely on one another to learn concepts, solve problems and complete projects (Kagan, 1986).

In cooperative learning, for instance, the students assist each other with drills and practice for material, for example, spelling words or math facts. Cooperative learning can involve teamwork to complete complex projects that require planning, research, and putting all the parts together.

In cooperative learning, there are more opportunities for students to communicate in a sense of cooperation than in more traditional settings. Also, in cooperative learning the quality of communication is higher as students try to understand the material in the content subjects. In cooperative learning there is a sense of cooperation exhibited as each participant has information that the other student needs.

In cooperative learning the students are provided with rich communication opportunities for limited English proficient students. An example of cooperative learning is Finding Out/Descubrimiento (Cohen, 1986). This uses science and math content to teach critical thinking skills. Students are assigned to talk groups with rotating roles such as facilitator, safety officer, and reporter. Groups work on problems in learning centers in areas such as optics, electricity, and water. Materials are provided in English and Spanish, and bilingual students serve as translators. Students can complete their assignments working in either language.

In cooperative learning primary language use is permitted in cooperative grouping, but the way this strategy works is that the dominant language—English—is more promoted so that it can be acquired more easily. Cooperative learning strategies might be classified as a second language teaching approach. Cooperative learning produces more opportunities for content-related communication among students in a more traditional teacher-centered classroom environment (Bowen, Madsen & Hilferty, 1985).

Cooperative strategies motivate students and promote a positive affective climate. These are the qualities which make dual language instruction so effective (Bowen, Madsen & Hilferty, 1985).

ENGLISH AS A SECOND LANGUAGE (ESL)

In reviewing the literature on the various bilingual methods, it became evident that there were not many articles written on ESL methodologies. After searching through several English as a second language materials, the writer discovered a few bilingual methods books which explained ESL methodology. In the section which follows, some of these ESL methods will be explained.

Various methodologies for second language teaching have been popular at different times.

Audiolingual Method

In audiolingualism, the process of learning a language is viewed as the acquisition of a set of habits which permit a speaker to respond correctly to a given stimulus. In order to acquire correct language habits, the learner must practice imitating language models and patterns until they can be produced automatically.

This method is based on a theory of behavioral psychology in which responses to different stimuli are drilled through practice and conditioning to become automatic habits. Language is seen as a series of patterns with transferable pieces. Various patterns are taught to the student so they can acquire these particular patterns. This approach was popular in the 1960s. Here the students memorize set dialogues, then manipulate sentences modeled by teachers in drills. As new research emerged on linguistic and psychological information in the 1970s, the popularity of the audiolingual approach diminished.

Since the 1970s, approaches that employ the selection of methods and techniques matched to the individual needs of the students have evolved. Emphasis has been placed on all four language skills—listening, reading, speaking, and writing—rather than just oral skills. Linguistic accuracy has been de-emphasized, and communication of meaning has been encouraged. Learner-centered activities have replaced teacher-directed drilling of correct sentence patterns.

Silent Way

In Silent Way instruction, the teacher points to color-coded symbols or letters on a wall chart that represent syllables in the students' native language (L_1). Students are encouraged to pronounce the syllables aloud as the teacher points to them. The teacher then switches to a similarly color-coded chart of symbols in the target language (TL). Students will read these syllables aloud using their knowledge of pronunciation in L_1 and of the color-coded system. When the students are ready, the teacher uses colored rods of different lengths, charts, and gestures to guide the students in producing more involved speech. Throughout these activities, the teacher directs learning while remaining silent most of the time.

This grammar-based approach reflects cognitive theory. Gattigno (1960) believes that learning is work that must be consciously done by the student. The students are often encouraged to transfer knowledge from L_1 to similar language tasks of the TL (Chamot 1984).

The Silent Way is a humanistic approach to second language instruction. Caleb Gattengno (1960) introduced this approach in 1963. This approach was not well-known until the mid-1970's. The theory behind the Silent Way is based on several general principles: (1) teaching is subordinate to learning; (2) students learn by listening to each other rather than teachers; and (3) greater progress is made through self-evaluation than through teacher evaluation (Chamot & McKeon, 1984). In this methodology wall charts and colored rods are used to establish the reference to meaning in the beginning levels of instruction.

Silence is used by both teachers and students to provide time for contemplating the sound and structure of the target language. Teachers point to a wall chart of symbols, which stand for syllables of spoken language and are color coded to indicate similar sound patterns represented by the symbols. Students at the beginning pronounce the syllables in the target language in a chorus, then pronounce the syllables individually. As students master the sound patterns of the target language, greater emphasis is placed on vocabulary development achieved through use of certain *specific* visual aids.

Counseling-Learning or Community Language Learning

Counseling-Learning or Community Learning was developed by Charles Curran in 1976, as a humanistic approach involving the learner's whole person through the use of counseling psychology techniques. In this approach teachers are the facilitators and the classroom emphasis is on shared, task-oriented activities where students and teachers cooperate in aiding each other. In the beginning, students sit in a circle and communicate freely with each other in their native languages. Teachers remain outside the circle and translate the conversation into the target language which the students repeat. Periods of silence and an unpressured atmosphere give students time to think about the language they are hearing. A tape of the session may be made and played at the end of the class. If students desire, teachers write all or part of the target language conversation and briefly explain its structure. The student is made to feel secure and is accepted in the classroom. The teacher's counseling skills and use of native language and translation in the early stages of the instruction are helpful to the student (Bowen, Madsen & Hilferty, 1985).

Counseling-Learning is also based on a theory of communication-competence in that students genuinely communicate with each other based on the relationships that have been established within the group (Bowen, Madsen & Hilferty, 1985).

Sugestopedia, Suggestopedy, and/or Suggestology

This method was developed by Bulgarian psychiatrist Georgi Lozanov. This approach is based on three principles: (1) students should enjoy rather than struggle against what they are doing, (2) students' conscious and unconscious reactions are inseparable; and (3) students' "reserve powers" must be mobilized leading to newer, faster, and more permanent kind of learning (Chamot & McKeon 1984).

The students are not threatened by or feel insecure with the new language through the planned use of non-verbal techniques, classical music, and comfortable aesthetic surroundings. The students are made to relax as they are learning the new language. Teachers also present the students with lengthy, culturally relevant dialogues. As was mentioned earlier, the teachers present much of this information with the use of classical music. After the students listen to the cultural dialogues, students interact with each other in the new language (Chamot, 1985).

Language Experience Approach

This English-as-a-second-language approach was developed by Van Allen and Allen in 1976.

This program was developed initially as a reading program for English-speaking children. This approach provides guided language experience in which students produce reading material based on their own interests and activities. They recount stories or describe pictures they have drawn. The teacher writes their words verbatim. These student-produced stories are used reading material and language development activities.

In this approach reading is viewed as an integral part of language. Very often in this approach students are excited to read their stories and often have little to no difficulty reading their own words which they can now see in print.

New Concurrent Approach

This approach was developed by Jacobson in 1981. In this method, there is an alternation in first and second languages. The teacher switches languages to reinforce concepts, lexical items, or cultural awareness and respond to dues initiated by the student. This approach to teaching is used in content classes. Jacobson believes that this approach provides sufficient input to facilitate acquisition of both languages. Duran (1991) completed some research involving more than 150 students with severe handicaps and autism and found that students learned best to do vocational tasks by the teacher speaking to the students in English and giving them some concept information or saying a few words about the concept or task they were to complete in their first language or Spanish. This was the first time such a study had been completed using this particular population.

Total Physical Response

This particular method was developed by Asher (1982). In the total physical response approach, (1) the teacher gives commands in the first language while simultaneously acting them out (2) the students demonstrate comprehension by correctly following the teacher commands. Simple commands (close the window) are made increasingly more complex (would you mind closing the window?). Students are not required to speak initially, but as speech emerges, they begin to give commands themselves.

The theory behind this approach is that a second language is best learned in the same manner and sequence as children learn their first language. Asher (1982) believes that listening should precede speaking. He also believes early language experiences should be linked to physical activity. Motivation is enhanced as this approach is used.

The Notational/Functional Syllabus

This approach was developed by (Van Ek 1977; Wilkins 1976). This method is viewed as a skill which can be used to accomplish functional tasks such as giving and receiving information, expressing opinions, and socializing. Students are taught what language does rather than how it works grammatically.

HOW BILINGUAL METHODS APPLY TO TEACHING STUDENTS WITH MODERATE AND SEVERE HANDICAPS

This writer has used several bilingual methods to teach students with severe disabilities. Many of the parents of the students without even realizing it often use similar methods to teach their son or daughter. Since parents find the native language comfortable and are fluent in the language they feel comfortable and secure in it. Thus teachers and professionals should encourage parents to speak their native language. As a caution when working in teaching another language, one should recall that some of the research or methodologies which tell us that it is extremely important that any phrase thought or sentences which are being communicated orally in one language not be interrupted by the speaker or another person in order to translate the sentence or phrase until the end of the sentence. If the translation is given before the person finishes speaking, the student may become confused and the effect of using the native language for translation will be extremely confusing to the learner. Thus attempting to speak a sentence in one language, then translating the thought immediately, is not an effective learning strategy, according to the research on effectively teaching second language learners. Even with more moderate to severe populations, this information would also be applicable.

The concurrent approach utilizes a dual approach to teaching concepts of second language learners. This approach can also be successfully utilized when teaching moderately to severely disabled learners. For example, when teaching students with autism or those with Down's syndrome (more moderately disabled), the trainer or teacher can say briefly in Spanish what the student is to do on the job, and then begin with English instruction of what the students are to do. As was noted earlier, it is important to finish speaking one thought in one language before beginning in the second language. Instruction with second language learners is more effective if each sentence or each word is not spoken in one language, then immediately translated in the second language. Doing this would be confusing, especially to more severe students who have a language and or communication disorder. Thus, give the concept in the students' native language, then proceeding with English, is helpful especially when teaching students concepts for the first time and is necessary in order for students to complete tasks.

Another approach used with second language learners who are more moderately to severely impaired is cooperative learning. In cooperative learning more fluent speakers in the native language and English as the second language are paired with students who are operating only in their first language or home language. When teaching these students who are more severely disabled and who are in need of hearing the concept spoken in the first language, it is important to look at which students are being paired together. If some students are paired together and one is more of a behavior problem than the other, it is a good idea to be sure that both students do not become ritualistic or begin showing an increase in tantruming behaviors. Placing two students together to help each other understand the concepts can be self-defeating in terms of one student modeling bad behavior for the other who is less severely impaired.

Another method that is often used with students of moderate to severe handicaps is the Natural Approach. In the Natural Approach the students are encouraged to be in small groups, and the teacher allows the student to talk concerning various topics. If a teacher of students with more moderate to severe disabilities uses some of this approach, students can be told to go over what they are going to purchase at the grocery stores, or students can go over in English what they are going to do when they cross the street.

The teacher can say for instance, "What are you going to buy at the store?" The students or student can respond, "Going to buy some juice." The fact that they are practicing English with topics of current activities they are going to do will be most helpful. If the students need, for instance, to hear their language to fully understand what they are going to say as they respond, then the teacher should say the idea or concept to the student in their first language briefly, then proceed with the activity or dialogue in English. For example, the teacher or trainer can say, "Vamos a la tienda." (We are going to the store). "¿Que vas a comprar?" (What are you going to buy?) The English portion of the conversation is not noted until the concept has briefly been given to the student in the student's native language. As has been noted before, this is done briefly and at the beginning of the instruction.

Students with moderate to more severe handicaps can enjoy talking and sharing with others in small groups and on a one-to-one basis. Even taking a walk in the neighborhood can result in things students can talk about in English with other students once the teacher leads them in conversation. Since many students with handicaps are not spontaneous, it is crucial that the teacher encourage the students to talk through various planned and functional activities.

Another approach that is part of English as a second language instruction is language experience. In language experience the students can be encouraged to once again talk about various activities they have done. For instance, some of the students may have gone to the community to make purchases. When they return, the teacher can go over briefly what was done, in·their first language. This activity of going over the material briefly in the students' native or home language helps students fully understand what will be communicated or completed in language$_2$ or the English language as in our case here.

After the teacher gives the students the concept of what was accomplished in the student's home or native language once, the student is asked to generate a title or even a phrase that will serve as the title of the story that the will be developed concerning the activity the student has participated in. The teacher or trainer will print on the board the words the student gives the teacher. The student will point to each word and say aloud what the student has indicated to the teacher.

The teacher asks the student further questions about the activity as the teacher writes what the student has indicated. Once again the student points to each word and says aloud each of the words. This procedure continues until a short functional story has been developed by the student. Since vocal students with moderate to severe handicaps do not often have a large vocabulary, the words they say to compile the story are often one or two word phrases. This is still helpful for the students because they will often see in print functional words; for instance, they may need to see words used at work, at home or in the community. Students enjoy reading functional stories of activities they have often participated in doing in the community. Photographs or realistic magazine pictures can be placed where the titles are so that attractive nice illustrations can accompany the stories they have shared with the teacher.

It has been this writer's experience that the language experience approach helps the students of limited English abilities not only feel good about themselves, because they can be successful reading materials, but the approach helps the student read functional words learned in the community or in his/her various environments.

Thus, there are many bilingual methods that are helpful and useful in teaching limited English proficient students who are moderately to severely disabled. Once the teacher or parent becomes familiar with these various useful approaches, they will realize that in some cases they have already been doing much instruction using these methods without even realizing that they were utilizing these approaches. The beauty of bilingual teaching techniques, as with other methods designed to teach students is that they are universal and can be used with all students in our classes.

It is unfortunate that not enough articles are written to explain more of the bilingual approaches or methods. As this writer was reading and preparing to write this chapter she became aware how simple and useful many bilingual methods are as she started to discover the techniques in various bilingual and English as a second language texts. The writer became excited to realize that many of the bilingual methods were methods that not only could be used with limited English proficient students but were methods that are often used in reading with regular education students. It is an amazing area of discovery if one can actually realize that all methods useful in one area and other disciplines can be carefully woven into teaching in other disciplines as in our case special education and are useful with all children. In the end what is important is to get any learner to understand the materials or concept. A good teacher borrows and uses varied approaches, and materials from all disciplines in order to make certain the child has learned the material that is being presented to him or her.

REFERENCES

Baca, L. (1984). Teacher Education Programs (In P. Chinn's, *Education of Culturally and Linguistically Different Exceptional Children*, ERIC Clearinghouse on Handicapped & Gifted Children, Council for Exceptional Children, pp. 101–123.

Block, E. (1986). The comprehension strategies of second language learners, *TESOL Quarterly*, Vol. 20, no. 3, pp. 463–464.

Bowen, J. Donald et al. (1980). An exploratory study on the Frequency of English Segmental Phonemes, in John F. Povey, ed, *Language Policy and Language Teaching: Essays in Honor of Clifford H. Prator*. Culver City, CA: English Language Services pp. 131–138.

Bowen, J. D., H. Madsen, & A. Hilferty (1985). *TESOL Techniques and Procedures*. Cambridge: Newberry House.

Castellanos, D. (1983). The best of two worlds: Bilingual bicultural education in the U.S. Trenton: New Jersey State Department of Education.

Chamot, Uhl A. & D. McKeon, (1984). *Educating the Minority Language Student: Classroom and Administrative Issues*, National Clearinghouse for Bilingual Education, Rosslyn, VA: InterAmerica Research Associates.

Chamot, Uhl, A. (1985). ESL Instructional Approaches and Underlying Language Learning Theories, *FOCUS: Thought Provoking Papers on Bilingual Education*, Rosslyn, VA: National Clearinghouse for Bilingual Education No. 20. pp. 1–4.

Chinn, P. C. (Ed.) (1984). *Education of Culturally and Linguistically Different Exceptional Children*, ERIC Clearinghouse on Handicapped and Gifted Children, Council for Exceptional Children.

Cummins, J. (1980). The cross-lingual dimensions of language proficiency: Implications for bilingual education and the optional age issue. *TESOL Quarterly*, 2, 175–187.

Dew, N. (1984). The Exceptional Bilingual Child: Demography, (In P. Chinn's (Ed.), *Education of Culturally and Linguistically Different Exceptional Children*, ERIC Clearinghouse on Handicapped & Gifted Children) pp. 1–41.

Durán, E. (1988). The effects of teaching English Only, Spanish Only and Spanish and English, *Reading Improvement*, Vol., No., pp.

Escamilla, K. (1980). German-English schools 1870–1917: Cultural and linguistic survival in St. Louis. *Bilingual Journal*, 5 (2), 16–20.

Esquivel, G. B. & R. K. Yoshida, (1985). Special Education for Language minority students, *Focus on Exceptional Children*, Vol. 18, No. 3, pp. 1–7.

Genesee, Fred (1985). Second language learning through immersion: A review of U.S. Programs, *Review of Educational Research*, Vol. 55, No. 4. pp. 541–561.

Gonzales, P. C. (1981). Beginning English reading for ESL students, *Reading Teacher*, pp. 154–162.

Graves, D. (1981). The growth and development of first grade writers. In D. Graves (Ed.), *A case study observing the development of primary children's composing, spelling, and motor behaviors during the writing process. Final Report.* Durham, NH: University of New Hampshire Press.

Gundlach, R. (1981). On the nature and development of children's writing. In C. Frederickson, M. Whiteman, & J. Dominic (Eds.), *Writing: The nature, development and teaching of written communication.* Hillsdale, NJ: Laurence, Erlbaum.

Gundlach, R. (1982). Children as writers: The beginning of learning to write. In M. Nystrand (Ed.), *What writers know: the language, process, and structure of written discourse.* New York: Academic Press.

Harste, J., C. Burke & V. Woodward (1983). Children's language and world: Initial encounters with print. (Final Report NIE–G 79-0132). Bloomington, IN: Language Education Departments.

Heath, S. (1983). *Ways with Words.* Cambridge: Cambridge University Press.

Horwitz, E. K. (1986). Some language acquisition principles about their implications for second language teaching, *Hispana,* Vol. 69, pp. 684–689.

Jacobson, R. (1987). "Allocating two languages as a key feature of a bilingual methodology." Paper presented at the meeting of the National Association for Bilingual Education, Denver, CO.

Lambert, W. (1983). Additive versus subtractive forms of bilingualism: Confusions regarding programs of immersion. In S. S. Seider (Ed.), *Issues of Language Assessment,* Springfield, IL: State Board of Education.

Lessow-Hurley, J. (1990). *The Foundations of Dual Language Instruction Lengua Langue Sprache Lingua,* New York: Longman.

Leung, E. K. (1989). Cultural and acculturational commonalities and diversities among Asian American: Identification and programming considerations, ERIC, (in A. Ortiz, and B. Ramirez's Schools and the *Culturally Diverse Exceptional Student: Promising Practices and Future Directions* pp. 86–95).

Long, M. H. (1983). Does second language instruction make a difference? A Review of the research, *TESOL Quarterly,* Vol. 17, No. 3, pp. 359–382.

MacNamara, J. A. (1966). *Bilingualism and primary education: A study of the Irish experience,* Edinburgh: Edinburgh University Press.

McLaughlin, Barry M. et al. (1989). Second language learning: An information processing perspective, *Language Learning,* Vol. 33, No. 2, pp. 135–158.

Milk, R. D. (1985). The Changing Role of ESL in Bilingual Education, *TESOL Quarterly,* Vol. 19, No. 4, pp. 657–672.

Modiano, N. (1986). National or mother tongue in beginning reading: A comparative study. *Research in the Teaching of English,* 2, 32–43.

Nutall, E. V., et al. (1984). A critical look at testing and evaluation from a Cross-cultural perspective. (In P. Chinn's (Ed.), *Education of Culturally and Linguistically Different Exceptional Children,* ERIC Clearinghouse on Handicapped and Gifted Children, pp. 42–59.

Omark, D. R., & J. G. Erickson, (1983). *The Bilingual Exceptional Child.* San Diego, CA: College Hill Press.

Ortiz, A. and B. Ramírez, (1989). *Schools and the Culturally Diverse Exceptional Students: Promising Practices and Future Directions,* ERIC Clearinghouse on Handicapped and Gifted Children.

Ovando, C. J. & V. P. Collier, (1985). Bilingual and ESL classrooms. New York: McGraw-Hill.

Perl, S. & N. Wilson, (1986). Through teachers' eyes: Portraits of writing teachers at work. New York: Heinemann.

Ratleff-Echevarria, J. & V. I. Graf, (1989), California Bilingual Special Education Model Sites (1984–1986). Programs and Research, *Schools & the Culturally Diverse Exceptional Student: Promising Practices and Future Directions*, pp. 104–111.

Reich, K. (1986). Hispanic population likely to double by 2020. *Austin American Statesman* A-4.

Samuels, D., & R. Griffore, (1979). The Plattsburgh French language immersion program: Its influence on intelligence and self esteem. *Language Learning*, Vol. 29, pp. 45–52.

Skutnabb-Kangas, T. (1984). *Bilingualism or not: The Education of Minorities.* Clevedon: Multilingual matters.

Tyack, D. B. (1974). *The one best system: A history of American urban education.* Cambridge, MA: Harvard University Press.

Van Ek, J. A. (1977). *The Threshold Level for Modern Language Learning in Schools.* The Council of Europe. London: Longman.

Weinberg, M. (1977). *A chance to learn: A history of race and education in the United States.* Cambridge: Cambridge University Press.

Wilkins, David A. (1976). *National Syllabuses.* London: Oxford University Press.

Williams, J. D. & G. C. Snipper, (1990). *Literacy and Bilingualism*, Longman, New York.

Yates, J. (1984). Demography as it Affects Special Education. [In P. Chinn's (Ed.), *Education of Culturally and Linguistically Different Exceptional Children,*] ERIC Clearinghouse on Handicapped & Gifted Children, pp. 1–5.

INDEX

Job coaches and trainers (*continued*)
   verbal cuing, 11
      use of children's primary language,
         15–16
      use of college students as, 13–19
   advantages of, 13
   introduction clients by slides, 16
   task analysis sheet, illustration, 15
   teaching parents of children, 14–15
   techniques used by, 13–14
      use of community persons as, 13–19
Job competence, 97
Job retention, 97
Job satisfaction, 97
Jobs and job training for students with
     autism, 88–90
     importance early training, 88
     jobs and job skills used, 89
     rotation students on various jobs, 89
     types jobs, 89
   charting job activities, 89–90
   tasks completed, 89
Johnson, B., 111, 116, 118, 120, 122
Johnson, S., 114, 121, 122
Jyack, 128

K

Kagan, 139
Kannet, Leo, 79
Karan, O. C., 110, 121, 122
Kennedy, C. H., 98, 99, 107, 121
Kishi, G., 105, 106, 122
Knight, C. B., 110, 121, 122
Koegel, R., 80, 95
Kregel, J., 46, 63

L

Lambert, W., 137, 149
Landrum, 130
Language, use of term, 130
Language Experience Approach to ESL, 143
Latino students and parents (*see also* Parents
   of autistic students)
   communication and/on gesturing
     instruction, 12
   cultural and linguistic considerations,
     75–76

   definition, 92
   number in U.S., 130
   parent attitude toward child with
     autism, 93–94
   role of religion, 94
   teaching of, 92–94
   use of term latino, 92
Lee, M., 114, 120, 121, 122
Lemare, 134
Lessow-Hurley, J., 125, 126, 127, 128, 132,
   138, 149
Leung, E.K., 149
Liability
   by school, 71
   during community-based activities,
     71–72
     automobile insurance coverages, 72
     use permission slips, 71–72
Liebert, D., 50, 62
Lignugaris/Kraft, B., 97, 111, 122, 123
Likins, M., 111, 122
Lily, William, 131
Lim, 131
Linguistic minority student, definition,
   130
Lipsky, D.K., 47, 48, 49, 51, 62
Locating community vocational training
     sites
   face-to-face contacts, 18
   ideas to help, 19–20
   jobs in food service, 21
   suggested sites, 20–22
   training people to assist in, 18
Long, M.H., 149
Lovaas, Ivar, 8, 25, 60, 63, 80, 81, 82, 84, 95
Lozanov, Georgi, 142
Lynch, K.P., 3, 25, 48

M

Macias, 131
MacNamara, J.A., 137, 149
Madsen, H., 132, 134, 135, 136, 140, 142, 148
Marger, M.N., 78
McCuller, G.L., 97, 123
McDonnell, J., 61, 63
McFall, R., 116, 122
McKeon, D., 141, 142, 148
McKinney, J.D., 48, 63

ENGLISH LANGUAGE INSTITUTE
LIBRARY
THE UNIVERSITY OF MICHIGAN

DATE DUE

GAYLORD   #3523PI   Printed in USA